Certificate Paper C2

FUNDAMENTALS OF
FINANCIAL ACCOUNTING

For assessments in 2010 and 2011

Practice & Revision Kit

In this December 2009 edition

- Banks of multiple choice questions and separate banks of objective test questions on every syllabus area
- Answers with detailed feedback
- Two mock assessments
- Fully up to date as at 1 December 2009

BPP Learning Media's **i-Pass** product also supports this paper

LEARNING MEDIA

First edition June 2006
Third edition December 2009

ISBN 9780 7517 8074 1
(previous 9780 7517 5181 9)

British Library Cataloguing-in-Publication Data
A catalogue record for this book
is available from the British Library

Published by

BPP Learning Media Ltd
BPP House, Aldine Place
London W12 8AA

www.bpp.com/learningmedia

Printed in the United Kingdom

Contents

Review form & free prize draw

Revising with this Kit

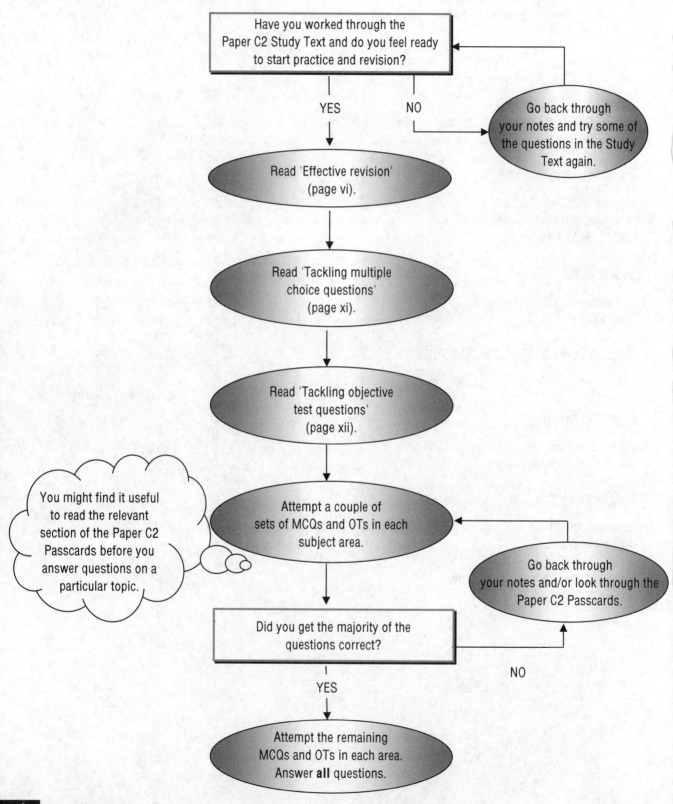

Have you worked through the Paper C2 Study Text and do you feel ready to start practice and revision?

YES · NO

Go back through your notes and try some of the questions in the Study Text again.

Read 'Effective revision' (page vi).

Read 'Tackling multiple choice questions' (page xi).

Read 'Tackling objective test questions' (page xii).

You might find it useful to read the relevant section of the Paper C2 Passcards before you answer questions on a particular topic.

Attempt a couple of sets of MCQs and OTs in each subject area.

Go back through your notes and/or look through the Paper C2 Passcards.

Did you get the majority of the questions correct?

YES · NO

Attempt the remaining MCQs and OTs in each area. Answer **all** questions.

BPP LEARNING MEDIA

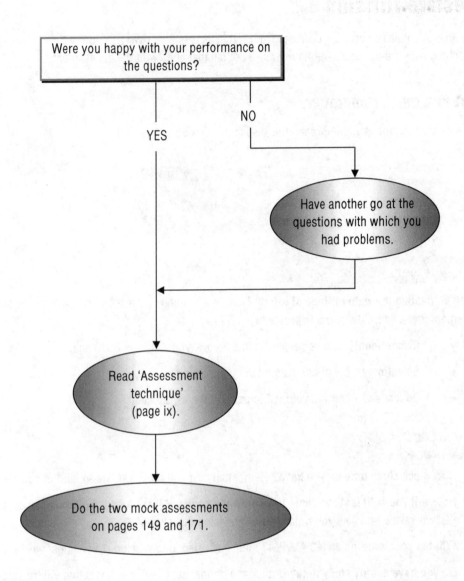

Were you happy with your performance on the questions?

YES

NO

Have another go at the questions with which you had problems.

Read 'Assessment technique' (page ix).

Do the two mock assessments on pages 149 and 171.

Effective revision

This guidance applies if you have been studying for an assessment over a period of time. (Some tuition providers are teaching subjects by means of one intensive course that ends with the assessment.)

What you must remember

Time is very important as you approach the assessment. You must remember:

> **Believe in yourself**
>
> **Use time sensibly**

Believe in yourself

Are you cultivating the right attitude of mind? There is absolutely no reason why you should not pass this **assessment** if you adopt the correct approach.

- **Be confident** – you've passed exams before, you can pass them again
- **Be calm** – plenty of adrenaline but no panicking
- **Be focused** – commit yourself to passing the assessment

Use time sensibly

1   **How much study time do you have?** Remember that you must **eat**, **sleep**, and of course, **relax**.

2   **How will you split that available time between each subject?** A revision timetable, covering what and how you will revise, will help you organise your revision thoroughly.

3   **What is your learning style?** AM/PM? Little and often/long sessions? Evenings/ weekends?

4   **Do you have quality study time?** Unplug the phone. Let everybody know that you're studying and shouldn't be disturbed.

5   **Are you taking regular breaks?** Most people absorb more if they do not attempt to study for long uninterrupted periods of time. A five minute break every hour (to make coffee, watch the news headlines) can make all the difference.

6   **Are you rewarding yourself for your hard work?** Are you leading a **healthy lifestyle?**

What to revise

You need to spend **most time** on, and practise **lots of questions** on, topics that are likely to yield plenty of questions in your assessment.

You may also find certain areas of the syllabus difficult.

Difficult areas are

- Areas you find dull or pointless
- Subjects you highlighted as difficult when you studied them
- Topics that gave you problems when you answered questions or reviewed the material

DON'T become depressed about these areas; instead do something about them.

- Build up your knowledge by **quick tests** such as the quick quizzes in your BPP Learning Media Study Text and the batches of questions in the i-Pass CD ROM.

- Work carefully through **examples** and **questions** in the Text, and refer back to the Text if you struggle with questions in the Kit.

Breadth of revision

Make sure your revision covers all areas of the syllabus. Your assessment will test your knowledge of the whole syllabus.

How to revise

There are four main ways that you can revise a topic area.

Write it!

Read it!

Teach it!

Do it!

Write it!

Writing important points down will help you recall them, particularly if your notes are presented in a way that makes it easy for you to remember them.

Read it!

You should read your notes or BPP Learning Media Passcards actively, testing yourself by doing quick quizzes or Kit questions while you are reading.

Teach it!

Assessments require you to show your understanding. Teaching what you are learning to another person helps you practise explaining topics that you might be asked to define in your assessment. Teaching someone who will challenge your understanding, someone for example who will be taking the same assessment as you, can be helpful to both of you.

Do it!

Remember that you are revising in order to be able to answer questions in the assessment. Practising questions will help you practise **technique** and **discipline**, which can be crucial in passing or failing assessments.

1   Start your question practice by doing a couple of sets of objective test questions in a subject area. Note down the questions where you went wrong, try to identify why you made mistakes and go back to your Study Text for guidance or practice.

2   The **more questions** you do, the more likely you are to pass the assessment. However if you do run short of time:

- Make sure that you have done at least some questions from every section of the syllabus
- Look through the banks of questions and do questions on areas that you have found difficult or on which you have made mistakes

3   When you think you can successfully answer questions on the whole syllabus, attempt the **two mock assessments** at the end of the Kit. You will get the most benefit by sitting them under strict assessment conditions, so that you gain experience of the vital assessment processes.

- Managing your time
- Producing answers

BPP Learning Media's *Learning to Learn Accountancy* gives further valuable advice on how to approach revision. BPP Learning Media has also produced other vital revision aids.

- **Passcards** – Provide you with clear topic summaries and assessment tips
- **i-Pass CDs** – Offer you tests of knowledge to be completed against the clock
- **MCQ cards** – Offer you practise in MCQs

You can purchase these products by visiting www.bpp.com/cima

Assessment technique

Format of the assessment

The assessment will contain 50 questions to be completed in 2 hours. The questions will be a combination of multiple choice questions and other types of objective test questions.

Passing assessments

Passing assessments is half about having the knowledge, and half about doing yourself full justice in the assessment. You must have the right approach to two things.

> ### The day of the assessment
> ### Your time in the assessment room

The day of the assessment

1   Set at least one **alarm** (or get an alarm call) for a morning assessment.

2   Have **something to eat** but beware of eating too much; you may feel sleepy if your system is digesting a large meal.

3   Allow plenty of **time to get to the assessment room**; have your route worked out in advance and listen to news bulletins to check for potential travel problems.

4   **Don't forget** pens and watch. Also make sure you remember **entrance documentation** and **evidence of identity**.

5   Put **new batteries** into your calculator and take a spare set (or a spare calculator).

6   **Avoid discussion** about the assessment with other candidates outside the assessment room.

Your time in the assessment room

1   **Listen carefully to the invigilator's instructions**

    Make sure you understand the formalities you have to complete.

2   **Ensure you follow the instructions on the computer screen**

    In particular ensure that you select the correct assessment (not every student does!), and that you understand how to work through the assessment and submit your answers.

3 Keep your eye on the time

In the assessment you will have to complete 50 questions in 120 minutes. That will mean that you have roughly 2½ minutes on average to answer each question. You will be able to answer some questions instantly, but others will require thinking about. If after a minute or so you have no idea how to tackle the question, leave it and come back to it later.

4 Label your workings clearly with the question number

This will help you when you check your answers, or if you come back to a question that you are unsure about.

5 Deal with problem questions

There are two ways of dealing with questions where you are unsure of the answer.

(a) **Don't submit an answer.** The computer will tell you before you move to the next question that you have not submitted an answer, and the question will be marked as not done on the list of questions. The risk with this approach is that you run out of time before you do submit an answer.

(b) **Submit an answer.** You can always come back and change the answer before you finish the assessment or the time runs out. You should though make a note of answers that you are unsure about, to ensure that you do revisit them later in the assessment.

6 Make sure you submit an answer for every question

When there are ten minutes left to go, concentrate on submitting answers for all the questions that you have not answered up to that point. You won't get penalised for wrong answers so take a guess if you're unsure.

7 Check your answers

If you finish the assessment with time to spare, check your answers before you sign out of the assessment. In particular revisit questions that you are unsure about, and check that your answers are in the right format and contain the correct number of words as appropriate.

BPP Learning Media's *Learning to Learn Accountancy* gives further valuable advice on how to approach the day of the assessment.

Tackling multiple choice questions

The MCQs in your assessment contain a number of possible answers. You have to **choose the option(s) that best answers the question**. The three incorrect options are called distracters. There is a skill in answering MCQs quickly and correctly. By practising MCQs you can develop this skill, giving you a better chance of passing the assessment.

You may wish to follow the approach outlined below, or you may prefer to adapt it.

Step 1   **Note down how long** you should allocate to each MCQ. For this paper you will be answering 50 questions in 120 minutes, so you will be spending on average just under two and a half minutes on each question. Remember however that you will not be expected to spend an equal amount of time on each MCQ; some can be answered instantly but others will take time to work out.

Step 2   **Attempt each question**. Read the question thoroughly.

You may find that you recognise a question when you sit the assessment. Be aware that the detail and/or requirement may be different. If the question seems familiar read the requirement and options carefully – do not assume that it is identical.

Step 3   Read the four options and see if one matches your own answer. Be careful with numerical questions, as the distracters are designed to match answers that incorporate **common errors**. Check that your calculation is correct. Have you followed the requirement exactly? Have you included every stage of a calculation?

Step 4   You may find that none of the options matches your answer.

- **Re-read the question** to ensure that you understand it and are answering the requirement
- **Eliminate any obviously wrong answers**
- **Consider which of the remaining answers** is the **most likely** to be correct and select the option

Step 5   If you are still unsure, **continue to the next question**. Likewise if you are nowhere near working out which option is correct after a couple of minutes, leave the question and come back to it later. Make a note of any questions for which you have submitted answers, but you need to return to later. The computer will list any questions for which you have not submitted answers.

Step 6   **Revisit questions** you are uncertain about. When you come back to a question after a break you often find you are able to answer it correctly straight away. If you are still unsure have a guess. You are not penalised for incorrect answers, so **never leave a question unanswered!**

Tackling objective test questions

What is an objective test question?

An objective test (**OT**) question is made up of some form of **stimulus**, usually a question, and a **requirement** to do something.

- **MCQs.** Read through the information on page (xi) about MCQs and how to tackle them.

- **True or false**. You will be asked if a statement is true or false.

- **Data entry**. This type of OT requires you to provide figures such as the correct figure for payables in a statement of financial position, or words to fill in a blank.

- **Multiple response.** These questions provide you with a number of options and you have to identify those that fulfil certain criteria.

OT questions in your assessment

CIMA is currently developing different types of OTs for inclusion in computer-based assessments. The timetable for introduction of new types of OTs is uncertain, and it is also not certain how many questions in your assessment will be MCQs, and how many will be other types of OT. Practising all the different types of OTs that this Kit provides will prepare you well for whatever questions come up in your assessment.

Dealing with OT questions

Again you may wish to follow the approach we suggest, or you may be prepared to adapt it.

Step 1   Work out **how long** you should allocate to each OT. Remember that you will not be expected to spend an equal amount of time on each one; some can be answered instantly but others will take time to work out.

Step 2   **Attempt each question**. Read the question thoroughly, and note in particular what the question says about the **format** of your answer and whether there are any **restrictions** placed on it (for example the number of words you can use).

           You may find that you recognise a question when you sit the assessment. Be aware that the detail and/or requirement may be different. If the question seems familiar read the requirement and options carefully – do not assume that it is identical.

Step 3   Read any options you are given and select which ones are appropriate. Check that your calculations are correct. Have you followed the requirement exactly? Have you included every stage of the calculation?

Step 4   You may find that you are unsure of the answer.

- Re-read the question to ensure that you understand it and are answering the requirement
- Eliminate any obviously wrong options if you are given a number of options from which to choose

Step 5   If you are still unsure, **continue to the next question**. Make a note of any questions for which you have submitted answers, but you need to return to later. The computer will list any questions for which you have not submitted answers.

Step 6   Revisit questions you are uncertain about. When you come back to a question after a break you often find you are able to answer it correctly straight away. If you are still unsure have a guess. You are not penalised for incorrect answers, so **never leave a question unanswered!**

Current issues

Feedback from students

Feedback from students sitting the CBAs has highlighted the following:

*   A mix of £ and $ may be used
*   Sales tax may be referred to as VAT

Useful websites

The websites below provide additional sources of information of relevance to your studies for *Fundamentals of Financial Accounting.*

*   BPP   www.bpp.com

    For details of other BPP material for your CIMA studies

*   CIMA   www.cimaglobal.com

    The official CIMA website

*   The Times   www.timesonline.co.uk
*   Financial Times   www.ft.com
*   The Economist   www.economist.com
*   Department of Trade and Industry   www.dti.gov.uk
*   UK Government   www.open.gov.uk

Question and Answer checklist/index

The headings in this checklist/index indicate the main topics of questions, but questions often cover several different topics.

Objective test questions

Multiple choice questions

1 Introduction to financial accounting

1   The *main* aim of accounting is to

      A   Maintain ledger accounts for every asset and liability
      B   Provide financial information to users of such information
      C   Produce a trial balance
      D   Record every financial transaction individually

2   In the time of rising prices, the historical cost convention has the effect of

      A   Understating profits and understating statement of financial position asset values
      B   Understating profits and overstating statement of financial position asset values
      C   Overstating profits and understating statement of financial position asset values
      D   Overstating profits and overstating statement of financial position asset values

3   Which of the following best explains what is meant by 'capital expenditure'?

     Capital expenditure is expenditure

      A   On non-current assets, including repairs and maintenance
      B   On expensive assets
      C   Relating to the issue of share capital
      D   Relating to the acquisition or improvement of non-current assets

4   Which of the following statements gives the best definition of the objective of accounting?

      A   To provide useful information to users
      B   To record, categorise and summarise financial transactions
      C   To calculate the taxation due to the government
      D   To calculate the amount of dividend to pay to shareholders

5   Which of the following is *not* an objective of financial statements?

      A   Providing information regarding the financial position of a business
      B   Providing information regarding the performance of a business
      C   Enabling users to assess the performance of management to aid decision making
      D   Helping to assess the going concern status of a business

6   Which of the following is *not* an information need for the 'Investor' group?

      A   Assessment of repayment ability of an entity
      B   Measuring performance, risk and return
      C   Taking decisions regarding holding investments
      D   Taking buy/sell decisions

2 Basic bookkeeping I

1 A credit balance of $917 brought down on Y's account in the books of X means that

A   X owes Y $917
B   Y owes X $917
C   X has paid Y $917
D   X is owed $917 by Y

2 A company received an invoice from ABC, for 40 units at $10 each, less 25% trade discount, these being items purchased on credit and for resale. It paid this invoice minus a cash discount of 2%. Which of the following journal entries correctly records the effect of the whole transaction in the company's books?

		Debit	Credit
		$	$
A	ABC	300	
	Purchases		300
	Cash	292	
	Discount allowed	8	
	ABC		300
B	Purchases	300	
	ABC		300
	ABC	300	
	Discount allowed		8
	Cash		292
C	Purchases	300	
	ABC		300
	ABC	300	
	Discount received		6
	Cash		294
D	ABC	400	
	Purchases		400
	Cash	294	
	Discount received	106	
	ABC		400

3 The following is an extract from the trial balance of ABC at 31 December 20X4.

	Debit	Credit
	$	$
Sales		73,716
Returns	5,863	3,492
Discounts	871	1,267

The figure to be shown in the trading account for net sales is

- A $66,586
- B $66,982
- C $67,853
- D $70,224

4 Which of the following would be recorded in the purchase day book?

- A Discounts received
- B Purchase invoices
- C Trade discounts
- D Credit notes received

5 The total of the sales day-book is recorded in the nominal ledger as:

	Debit	Credit
A	Receivables	Receivables Control Account
B	Receivables Control Account	Receivables
C	Sales Account	Receivables Control Account
D	Receivables Control Account	Sales Account

6 Which of the following postings from the cashbook payments side is wrong?

- A The total of the cash paid column to the debit of the cash control account.
- B The total of the discounts column to the credit of the discounts received account.
- C The total of the discounts column to the debit of the payables control account.
- D The total of the cash paid column to the credit of the cash control account.

7 (i) A debit entry in the cashbook will increase an overdraft.
  (ii) A debit entry in the cashbook will increase a bank balance.

Are these statements true?

- A Both true
- B Both false
- C (i) true and (ii) false
- D (i) false and (ii) true

8   A business sells goods costing $200 plus sales tax at 17.5%. Which of the following entries correctly records this *credit sale*?

A	Dr	Receivables	$235	
	Cr	Sales		$235
B	Dr	Receivables	$200	
	Cr	Sales		$165
	Cr	Sales tax a/c		$35
C	Dr	Receivables	$235	
	Cr	Sales		$200
	Cr	Sales tax a/c		$35
D	Dr	Sales	$200	
	Dr	Sales tax	$35	
	Cr	Payables		$235

9   A credit balance on a ledger account indicates

A   An asset or an expense
B   A liability or an expense
C   An amount owing to the organisation
D   A liability or a revenue

10   Which ONE of the following is not a book of prime entry?

A   The petty cash book
B   The sales returns day book
C   The sales ledger
D   The cash book

3 Basic bookkeeping II

1   A book of prime entry is one in which

A   The rules of double-entry bookkeeping do not apply
B   Ledger accounts are maintained
C   Transactions are entered prior to being recorded in the ledger account
D   Subsidiary accounts are kept

2 The double-entry system of bookkeeping normally results in which of the following balances on the ledger accounts?

	Debit balances	Credit balances
A	Assets and revenues	Liabilities, capital and expenses
B	Revenues, capital and liabilities	Assets and expenses
C	Assets and expenses	Liabilities, capital and revenues
D	Assets, expenses and capital	Liabilities and revenues

3 A sole trader had opening capital of $10,000 and closing capital of $4,500. During the period, the owner introduced capital of $4,000 and withdrew $8,000 for her own use.

Her profit or loss during the period was

A $9,500 loss
B $1,500 loss
C $7,500 profit
D $17,500 profit

4 A credit entry of $450 on X's account in the receivables ledger of Y could have arisen by

A X buying goods on credit from Y
B Y paying X $450
C Y returning goods to X
D X returning goods to Y

4 Concepts

1 The historical cost convention

A Fails to take account of changing price levels over time
B Records only past transactions
C Values all assets at their cost to the business, without any adjustment for depreciation
D Has been replaced in accounting records by a system of current cost accounting

2 The accounting convention under which items in the accounts are adjusted by reference to the Retail Price Index is known as

A Current cost accounting
B Historical cost accounting
C Alternative accounting rules
D Current purchasing power accounting

3   The accounting equation can be rewritten as

    A   Assets plus profit less drawings less liabilities equals closing capital
    B   Assets less liabilities less drawings equals opening capital plus profit
    C   Assets less liabilities less opening capital plus drawings equals profit
    D   Opening capital plus profit less drawings less liabilities equals assets

4   If the owner of a business takes goods from inventory for his own personal use, the accounting concept to be considered is the

    A   Prudence concept
    B   Capitalisation concept
    C   Money measurement concept
    D   Separate entity concept

5   Sales revenue should be recognised when goods and services have been supplied; costs are incurred when goods and services have been received.

    The accounting concept which governs the above is the

    A   Accruals concept
    B   Materiality concept
    C   Realisation concept
    D   Dual aspect concept

6   The capital maintenance concept implies that

    A   The capital of a business should be kept intact by not paying out dividends

    B   A business should invest its profits in the purchase of capital assets

    C   Non-current assets should be properly maintained

    D   Profit is earned only if the value of an organisation's net assets or its operating capability has increased during the accounting period

7   In times of rising prices, the historical cost convention:

    A   Understates asset values and profits
    B   Understates asset values and overstates profits
    C   Overstates asset values and profits
    D   Overstates asset values and understates profits

8   Which of the following is *not* an accounting concept?

    A   Prudence
    B   Consistency
    C   Depreciation
    D   Accruals

9   Making bad debt provisions and valuing inventory on the same basis in each accounting period are examples of which accounting concepts?

	Bad debt provision	Inventory valuation
A	Accruals	Consistency
B	Accruals	Going concern
C	Prudence	Consistency
D	Prudence	Going concern

10   The prudence concept means that profit is only included in the income statement if it is:

A   Expected
B   Material
C   Realised
D   Received

11   Which basic accounting concept is being followed when a charge is made for depreciation?

A   Accruals
B   Consistency
C   Going concern
D   Prudence

12   If, at the end of the financial year, a company makes a charge against the profits for stationery consumed but not yet invoiced, this adjustment is in accordance with the concept of

A   Materiality
B   Accruals
C   Consistency
D   Objectivity

5 Accruals and prepayments

1   Rent paid on 1 October 20X2 for the year to 30 September 20X3 was $1,200, and rent paid on 1 October 20X3 for the year to 30 September 20X4 was $1,600.

Rent payable, as shown in the income statement for the year ended 31 December 20X3, would be

A $1,200
B $1,600
C $1,300
D $1,500

2   Stationery paid for during 20X5 amounted to $1,350. At the beginning of 20X5 there was an inventory of stationery on hand of $165 and an outstanding invoice for $80. At the end of 20X5, there was an inventory of stationery on hand of $140 and an outstanding invoice for $70. The stationery figure to be shown in the income statement for 20X5 is

A $1,195
B $1,335
C $1,365
D $1,505

3   A business received or issues the following invoices and pays or received the invoiced amounts on the following dates:

	Invoice date	Invoice amount	Date paid or received
Purchase	2.6.X1	$200	26.6.X1
	25.6.X1	$300	2.7.X1
Sales	8.6.X1	$400	26.6.X1
	29.6.X1	$600	7.7.X1

There is no inventory at the beginning or end of June.

What is the difference between the profit for June calculated on a cash basis, and calculated on an accruals basis?

A   Nil
B $200
C $300
D $500

4   During the year, $4,000 was paid to the electricity board. At the beginning of the year, $1,000 was owed, and at the end of the year $1,200 was owed?

What is the charge for electricity in the year's income statement?

A $3,000
B $4,000
C $4,200
D $5,200

5   On 7 November 20X1, $8,400 rent was paid for the 24 months to 31 September 20X3.

What is the charge for rent in the income statement and the statement of financial position (SOFP) entry for the year to 31 December 20X2?

	Income statement	SOFP
A	$4,200	Prepayment $3,150
B	$4,200	Prepayment $4,200
C	$5,250	Accrual $3,150
D	$5,250	Accrual $4,200

6   During the year $5,000 rent was received. At the beginning of the year, the tenant owed $1,000, at the end of the year the tenant owed $500.

What is the rent received figure for the year's income statement?

A $4,000
B $4,500
C $5,000
D $5,500

7   During the year, $4,000 was paid for motor expenses. At the end of the year, the charge in the income statement was $5,000, with an accrual of $2,500 in the statement of financial position.

What was in last year's statement of financial position for motor vehicles?

A   Accrual $1,500
B   Prepayment $1,500
C   Accrual $3,500
D   Prepayment $3,590

8   At 1 September, the motor expenses account showed 4-months' insurance prepaid of $80 and petrol accrued of $95. During September, the outstanding petrol bill is paid, plus further bills of $245. At 30 September there is a further outstanding petrol bill of $120.

The amount to be shown in the income statement for motor expenses for September is

A $385
B $415
C $445
D $460

9   A tenant pays us rent of $1,000 a month. At the year-end he had paid 3 months in advance. During the year, $16,000 was received.

What was in our last year's statement of financial position in respect of this tenant?

A $1,000 debit
B $1,000 credit
C $7,000 debit
D $7,000 credit

10   Which **one** of the following statements is true?

A   Bad debts are an example of a prepayment
B   Prepayments are current liabilities
C   Prepayments decrease the profit in the income statement
D   Prepayments are included in current assets in the statement of financial position

6 Non-current assets I

1   What is the purpose of charging depreciation in accounts?

   A   To allocate the cost less residual value of a non-current asset over the accounting periods expected to benefit from its use

   B   To ensure that funds are available for the eventual replacement of the asset

   C   To reduce the cost of the asset in the statement of financial position to its estimated market value

   D   To comply with the prudence concept

2   Your firm bought a machine for $5,000 on 1 January 20X1, which had an expected useful life of four years and an expected residual value of $1,000; the asset was to be depreciated on the straight-line basis. On 31 December 20X3, the machine was sold for $1,600.

The amount to be entered in the 20X3 income statement for profit or loss on disposal, is

   A   Profit of $600
   B   Loss of $600
   C   Profit of $350
   D   Loss of $400

3   A non-current asset register showed a net book value of $67,460. A non-current asset costing $15,000 had been sold for $4,000, making a loss on disposal of $1,250. No entries had been made in the non-current asset register for this disposal.

The balance on the non-current asset register should be

   A $42,710
   B $51,210
   C $53,710
   D $62,210

4   An organisation's non-current asset register shows a net book value of $135,600. The non-current asset account in the nominal ledger shows a net book value of $125,600. The difference could be due to a disposed asset not having been removed from the non-current asset register.

   A   With disposal proceeds of $15,000 and a profit on disposal of $5,000
   B   With disposal proceeds of $15,000 and a net book value of $5,000
   C   With disposal proceeds of $15,000 and a loss on disposal of $5,000
   D   With disposal proceeds of $5,000 and a net book value of $5,000

5   Recording the purchase of computer stationery by debiting the computer equipment account at cost would result in

   A   An overstatement of profit and an overstatement of non-current assets
   B   An understatement of profit and an overstatement of non-current assets
   C   An overstatement of profit and an understatement of non-current assets
   D   An understatement of profit and an understatement of non-current assets

6   Depreciation is best described as

   A   A means of spreading the payment for non-current assets over a period of years
   B   A decline in the market value of the assets
   C   A means of spreading the net cost of non-current assets over their estimated useful life
   D   A means of estimating the amount of money needed to replace the assets

7   A business has made a profit of $8,000 but its bank balance has fallen by $5,000. This could be due to

   A   Depreciation of $3,000 and an increase in inventory of $10,000
   B   Depreciation of $6,000 and the repayment of a loan of $7,000
   C   Depreciation of $12,000 and the purchase of new non-current assets for $25,000
   D   The disposal of a non-current asset for $13,000 less than its book value

8   A non-current asset costing $12,500 was sold at a book loss of $4,500. Depreciation had been provided using the reducing balance, at 20% per annum since its purchase.

   Which of the following correctly describes the sale proceeds and length of time for which the asset had been owned?

	Sale proceeds	Length of ownership
A	Cannot be calculated	Cannot be calculated
B	Cannot be calculated	2 years
C	$8,000	Cannot be calculated
D	$8,000	2 years

9   On 1 July 20X7, your non-current asset register showed a net book value of $47,500. The ledger accounts showed non-current assets at cost of $60,000 and accumulated depreciation of $15,000. It was discovered that the disposal of an asset for $4,000, giving rise to a loss on disposal of $1,500, had not been recorded in the non-current asset register.

   After correcting this omission, the non-current asset register would show a balance which was

   A $3,000 lower than the ledger accounts
   B $1,500 lower than the ledger accounts
   C   equal to the ledger accounts
   D $1,000 higher than the ledger accounts

10   A non-current asset was purchased at the beginning of Year 1 for $2,400 and depreciated by 20% per annum
      by the reducing balance method. At the beginning of Year 4 it was sold for $1,200. The result of this was

      A   A loss on disposal of $240.00
      B   A loss on disposal of $28.80
      C   A profit on disposal of $28.80
      D   A profit on disposal of $240.00

7 Non-current assets II

1   The net book value of a company's non-current assets was $200,000 at 1 August 20X8. During the year ended 31
      July 20X9, the company sold non-current assets for $25,000 on which it made a loss of $5,000. The depreciation
      charge for the year was $20,000. What was the net book value of non-current assets at 31 July 20X9?

      A $150,000
      B $155,000
      C $160,000
      D $180,000

2   Which of the following costs would be classified as capital expenditure for a restaurant business?

      A   A replacement for a broken window
      B   Repainting the restaurant
      C   An illuminated sign advertising the business name
      D   Knives and forks for the restaurant

3   On 1 June 20X9 a machine was sold which cost $20,000 on 31 July 20X5. The sale proceeds were $5,500.
      The depreciation policy for machinery is 20% pa straight line, with a full year being charged in the year of
      acquisition and none in the year of disposal. The year-end is 31 December.

      What is the profit or loss on disposal?

      A   Profit $834
      B   Loss $834
      C   Profit $1,500
      D   Loss $1,500

4   On 1 June 20X9 a machine was sold which cost $20,000 on 31 July 20X5. Sale proceeds were $5,500 and
      the profit on disposal was $1,500. The depreciation policy for machinery is straight line with a full year being
      charged in the year of acquisition and none in the year of sale.

      What is the depreciation rate?

      A   20% pa
      B   25% pa
      C   30% pa
      D   35% pa

5   A business buys a machine for $15,000. The depreciation policy for machinery is 15% pa reducing balance. What is the net book value of the machine after two years of use?

 A $10,500
 B $10,837
 C $11,175
 D $12,750

6   A company has recorded its freehold property at its historical cost of $100,000. It now decides to record it at its market value of $280,000, by making which entries?

 A Debit non-current assets 180,000
   Credit revaluation reserve   180,000

 B Debit revaluation reserve 180,000
   Credit non-current assets   180,000

 C Debit non-current assets 180,000
   Credit income statement   180,000

 D Debit non-current assets 280,000
   Credit revaluation reserve   280,000

7   Which of the following would not be included in intangible non-current assets in a company's financial statements?

 A Development costs
 B Goodwill
 C Patents
 D Shares held in a supplier

8 Bad debts and allowances for receivables

1   A decrease in the allowance for receivables would result in

 A An increase in liabilities
 B A decrease in working capital
 C A decrease in net profit
 D An increase in net profit

2   A company has been notified that a receivable has been declared bankrupt. The company had previously provided for this doubtful debt. Which of the following is the correct double entry?

	DR	CR
A	Bad debts account	The receivable
B	The receivable	Bad debt account
C	Allowance for receivables	The receivable
D	The receivable	Allowance for receivables

3   An increase in an allowance for receivables has been treated as a reduction in the financial statements. The amount is $8,000. Which of the following explains the resulting effects?

    A   Net profit is overstated by $16,000, receivables overstated by $8,000
    B   Net profit understated by $16,000, receivables understated by $16,000
    C   Net profit overstated by $16,000, receivables overstated by $16,000
    D   Gross profit overstated by $16,000, receivables overstated by $16,000

4   At 1 January 20X1, there was an allowance for receivables of $3,000. During the year, $1,000 of debts was written off, and $800 of bad debts was recovered. At 31 December 20X1, it was decided to adjust the allowance for receivables to 5% of receivables which are $20,000.

What is the total bad debt expense for the year?

    A $200 debit
    B $1,800 debit
    C $2,200 debit
    D $1,800 credit

5   At the beginning of the year, allowance for receivables was $1,000. At the end of the year when receivables were $18,500, a specific allowance was made for the whole of Bert's debt of $500 and for 80% of Fred's debt of $1,000. It was decided to make a general allowance of 2% of remaining debts.

What was the closing balance on the allowance for receivables account?

    A $640
    B $1,640
    C $1,644
    D $2,640

6   Allowances for receivables are an example of which accounting concept?

    A   Accruals
    B   Consistency
    C   Matching
    D   Prudence

7   At the beginning of the year, the allowance for receivables was $850. At the year-end, the allowances required was $1,000. During the year $500 of debts were written off, which includes $100 previously included in the allowance for receivables.

What is the charge to income statement for bad debts and allowance for receivables for the year?

    A $1,500
    B $1,000
    C $650
    D $550

9 Cost of goods sold and inventories I

1   Gross profit for 20X3 can be calculated from

A   Purchases for 20X3, plus inventory at 31 December 20X3, less inventory at 1 January 20X3
B   Purchases for 20X3, less inventory at 31 December 20X3, plus inventory at 1 January 20X3
C   Cost of goods sold during 20X3, plus sales during 20X3
D   Net profit for 20X3, plus expenses for 20X3

2   A trial balance contains the following:

	$
Opening inventory	1,000
Closing inventory	2,000
Purchases	10,000
Purchases returned	200
Carriage inwards	1,500
Prompt payment discounts received	800

What is the cost of sales figure?

A $8,800
B $9,500
C $10,300
D $12,300

3   In times of rising prices, the FIFO method of inventory valuation, when compared to the average cost method of inventory valuation, will usually produce

A   A higher profit and a lower closing inventory value
B   A higher profit and a higher closing inventory value
C   A lower profit and a lower closing inventory value
D   A lower profit and a higher closing inventory value

4   Following the preparation of the income statement, it is discovered that accrued expenses of $1,000 have been ignored and that closing inventory has been overvalued by $1,300. This will have resulted in

A   An overstatement of net profit of $300
B   An understatement of net profit of $300
C   An overstatement of net profit of $2,300
D   An understatement of net profit of $2,300

5   Inventory is valued using FIFO. Opening inventory was 10 units at $2 each. Purchases were 30 units at $3 each, then issues of 12 units were made, followed by issues of 8 units.

Closing inventory is valued at

A $50
B $58
C $60
D $70

6   An organisation's inventory at 1 July is 15 units @ $3.00 each. The following movements occur:

- 3 July 20X6   5 units sold at $3.30 each
- 8 July 20X6   10 units bought at $3.50 each
- 12 July 20X6   8 units sold at $4.00 each

Closing inventory at 31 July, using the FIFO method of inventory valuation would be

A $31.50
B $36.00
C $39.00
D $41.00

7   Your organisation uses the weighted average cost method of valuing inventories. During August 20X1, the following inventory details were recorded:

Opening balance	30 units valued at $2 each
5 August	purchase of 50 units at $2.40 each
10 August	issue of 40 units
18 August	purchase of 60 units at $2.50 each
23 August	issue of 25 units

The value of the balance at 31 August 20X1 was

A $172.50
B $176.25
C $180.00
D $187.50

8   During September, your organisation had sales of $148,000, which made a gross profit of $40,000. Purchases amounted to $100,000 and opening inventory was $34,000.

The value of closing inventory was

A $24,000
B $26,000
C $42,000
D $54,000

9   Your firm values inventory using the weighted average cost method. At 1 October 20X8, there were 60 units in inventory valued at $12 each. On 8 October , 40 units were purchased for $15 each, and a further 50 units were purchased for $18 each on 14 October. On 21 October, 75 units were sold for $1,200.

The value of closing inventory at 31 October 20X8 was:

A $900
B $1,020
C $1,110
D $1,125

---

10   Inventory movements for product X during the last quarter were as follows:

January	Purchases	10 items at $19.80 each
February	Sales	10 items at $30 each
March	Purchases	20 items at $24.50 each
	Sales	5 items at $30 each

Opening inventory at 1 January was 6 items valued at $15 each

Gross profit for the quarter, using the weighted average cost method, would be

A $135.75
B $155.00
C $174.00
D $483.00

---

10 Cost of goods sold and inventories II

1   In times of rising prices, the valuation of inventory using the FIFO method, as opposed to average cost, will result in which ONE of the following combinations?

	Cost of sales	Profit	Closing inventory
A	Lower	Higher	Higher
B	Lower	Higher	Lower
C	Higher	Lower	Higher
D	Higher	Higher	Lower

---

2   Which of the following methods of valuing inventory are allowed under IAS 2?

(i)   LIFO
(ii)   Average cost
(iii) FIFO
(iv)   Replacement cost

A   (i), (ii), (iii), (iv)
B   (i), (ii), (iv)
C   (ii), (iii)
D   (iii), (iv)

3   Opening inventory of raw materials was $58,000, closing inventory was $63,000, purchases were $256,000, purchase returns were $17,000. What was cost of sales?

   A $256,000
   B $234,000
   C $239,000
   D $244,000

4   How should a loss of inventory (value $15,000) caused by flooding in the company's warehouse be accounted for? (Assume the inventory loss is not insured.)

   A   Dr   Trading a/c $15,000
           Cr   I/S a/c $15,000

   B   Dr   I/S a/c $15,000
           Cr   Trading a/c $15,000

   C   Dr   Drawings $15,000
           Cr   Trading a/c $15,000

   D   Dr   Inventory a/c $15,000
           Cr   Trading a/c $15,000

5   Net realisable value means? (In relation to the valuation of inventory.)

   A   The expected selling price of the inventory.

   B   The expected selling price less disposals costs less, in the case of incomplete items, the cost of completion.

   C   The replacement cost of the inventory.

   D   The market price.

6   FIFO, LIFO and average cost are inventory valuation methods. Which of the following statements is correct?

   A   When prices are rising FIFO will produce the higher profit figure of all these methods.
   B   When prices are rising LIFO will produce the higher profit figure of all these methods.
   C   LIFO is a permissible valuation method under IAS 2.
   D   Average cost is recomputed following every dispatch or issue of inventory.

7   A company has an annual inventory count, the factory did not cease production during the inventory count and some goods in work in progress (cost $5,500) were later counted again and included in finished goods inventory (cost $7,500). As a result profit was?

   A   Overstated by $2,000
   B   Overstated by $7,500
   C   Overstated by $5,500
   D   Overstated by $13,000

8 Which of the following statements are correct?

(i) A inventory valuation should include carriage in.
(ii) A inventory valuation should exclude carriage out.

A Both correct
B Both incorrect
C (i) correct, (ii) incorrect
D (i) incorrect, (ii) correct

9 A company which gives its sales personnel 5% of sales price as commission, has this inventory at the year end:

	Quantity	Cost	Per unit Estimated sales price
Beads	2,000	$1.50	$1.53
Buttons	1,500	$1.25	$1.40
Bows	2,000	$1.60	$1.50

At what value should this inventory be recorded in the financial statements?

A $7,756
B $7,632
C $7,875
D $8,175

11 Bank reconciliations I

1 Your cash book at 31 December 20X3 shows a bank balance of $565 overdrawn. On comparing this with your bank statement at the same date, you discover the following.

(a) A cheque for $57 drawn by you on 29 December 20X3 has not yet been presented for payment.

(b) A cheque for $92 from a customer, which was paid into the bank on 24 December 20X3, has been dishonoured on 31 December 20X3.

The correct bank balance to be shown in the statement of financial position at 31 December 20X3 is

A $714 overdrawn
B $657 overdrawn
C $473 overdrawn
D $53 overdrawn

2   The cash book shows a bank balance of $5,675 overdrawn at 31 August 20X5. It is subsequently discovered that a standing order for $125 has been entered twice, and that a dishonoured cheque for $450 has been debited in the cash book instead of credited.

The correct bank balance should be

A $5,100 overdrawn
B $6,000 overdrawn
C $6,250 overdrawn
D $6,450 overdrawn

3   A business had a balance at the bank of $2,500 at the start of the month. During the following month, it paid for materials invoiced at $1,000 less trade discount of 20% and cash discount of 10%. It received a cheque from a receivable in respect of an invoice for $200, subject to cash discount of 5%.

The balance at the bank at the end of the month was

A $1,970
B $1,980
C $1,990
D $2,000

4   The bank statement on 31 October 20X7 showed an overdraft of $800. On reconciling the bank statement, it was discovered that a cheque drawn by your company for $80 had not been presented for payment, and that a cheque for $130 from a customer had been dishonoured on 30 October 20X7.

The correct bank balance to be shown in the statement of financial position at 31 October 20X7 is

A $1,010 overdrawn
B $880 overdrawn
C $750 overdrawn
D $720 overdrawn

5   Your firm's cash book at 30 April 20X8 shows a balance at the bank of $2,490. Comparison with the bank statement at the same date reveals the following differences:

	$
Unpresented cheques	840
Bank charges not in cash book	50
Receipts not yet credited by the bank	470
Dishonoured cheque not in cash book	140

The correct balance on the cash book at 30 April 20X8 is

A $1,460
B $2,300
C $2,580
D $3,140

6 Your firm's bank statement at 31 October 20X8 shows a balance of $13,400. You subsequently discover that the bank has dishonoured a customer's cheque for $300 and has charged bank charges of $50, neither of which is recorded in your cash book. There are unpresented cheques totalling $2,400. Amounts paid in, but not yet credited by the bank, amount to $1,000. You further discover that an automatic receipt from a customer of $195 has been recorded as a credit in your cash book.

Your cash book balance, prior to correcting the errors and omissions, was:

A $11,455
B $11,960
C $12,000
D $12,155

7 Your firm's cashbook shows a credit bank balance of $1,240 at 30 April 20X9. Upon comparison with the bank statement, you determine that there are unpresented cheques totalling $450, and a receipt of $140 which has not yet been passed through the bank account. The bank statement shows bank charges of $75 which have not been entered in the cash book.

The balance on the bank statement is

A $1,005 overdrawn
B $930 overdrawn
C $1,475
D $1,550

8 Which of the following is NOT a valid reason for the cash book and bank statement failing to agree?

A   Timing difference
B   Bank charges
C   Error
D   Cash receipts posted to payables

9 The bank statement at 31 December 20X1 shows a balance of $1,000. The cash book shows a balance of $750 in hand. Which of the following is the most likely reason for the difference.

A   Receipts of $250 recorded in cash book, but not yet recorded by bank
B   Bank charges of $250 shown on the bank statement, not in the cash book
C   Standing orders of $250 included on bank statement, not in the cash book
D   Cheques for $250 recorded in the cash book, but not yet gone through the bank account

10 The cash book balance at 30 November 20X2 shows an overdraft of $500. Cheques for $6,000 have been written and sent out, but do not yet appear on the bank statement. Receipts of $5,000 are in the cash book, but are not yet on the bank statement. What is the balance on the bank statement?

A $1,500
B $500 in hand
C $1,500 in hand
D $500 overdrawn

12 Bank reconciliations II

1   A debit entry on a bank statement will have which effect on the level of a bank overdraft and a bank balance?

	Bank overdraft	Bank balance
A	Increase	Increase
B	Decrease	Decrease
C	Increase	Decrease
D	Decrease	Increase

2   When preparing a bank reconciliation it is realised that:

(i)   Cheques with a value of $1,050 have been sent to suppliers and correctly entered in the cash book, but have not yet been presented for payment.

(ii)   A cheque for $75 sent to a supplier has been incorrectly recorded in the cash book as $57.

(iii)   Before correction, the cash book has a balance of $10,500 credit.

(iv)   Bank charges of $175 have not been recorded in the cash book.

The balance of the cashbook after the correction is:

A $10,307 overdrawn
B $10,343 overdrawn
C $10,657 overdrawn
D $10,693 overdrawn

3   When preparing a bank reconciliation, it is realised that:

(i)   Cheques with a value of $1,050 have been sent to suppliers and correctly entered in the cash book, but have not yet been presented for payment.

(ii)   A cheque for $75 sent to a supplier has been incorrectly recorded in the cash book as $57.

(iii)   Before correction, the cash book has a balance of $10,500 credit.

(iv)   Bank charges of $175 have not been recorded in the cash book.

What is the closing balance shown on the bank statement?

A $9,257 overdrawn
B $9,643 overdrawn
C $11,357 overdrawn
D $11,743 overdrawn

4   When preparing a bank reconciliation, it is realised that:

    (i)   There are unpresented cheques of $8,000
    (ii)   There are lodgements of $5,000 uncleared
    (iii)   Bank charges of $67 have not been recorded in the cash book

What adjustment is required to the cash account?

    A   Debit $67
    B   Credit $67
    C   Debit $3,067
    D   Credit $3,067

---

5   A company uses the imprest system to control its petty cash, keeping a float of $50.

Since the cash was last replenished it had the following transactions:

    1    $12.50 to the milkman
    2    $10.00 on taxis
    3    $5.70 on stationary
    4    $20 advance taken by the director for a taxi fare last week returned unused
    5    $18.50 to the cleaner
    6    $15 advance to the MD's secretary

How much should now be drawn out of the bank?

    A $50
    B $41.70
    C $46.70
    D $31.70

---

6   A business has the following cash and bank transactions during January 20X1. Balance 1.1.20X1: cash $500, bank $1,000 overdrawn, receipts of cash $12,600, cash paid $3,200, cash paid to bank $5,500, payments by cheque $8,200. Closing balances: cash $600, bank $6,200 overdrawn. Calculate the total cash and bank drawings.

    A $14,800 (no bank drawings)
    B $860
    C $11,800
    D $6,300

---

7   A company has an opening cash book balance of $5,000 debit. During the month receivables paid $26,000, cash sales were $2,500 and payments were made to payables of $12,000 less 2% cash discounts. A comparison with the bank statement showed $125 bank charges had not been recorded in the cash book. What is the adjusted cash book balance?

    A $21,855 credit
    B $21,615 debit
    C $21,375 debit
    D $18,875 credit

13 Control accounts, sales tax and payroll I

1   From the following information, calculate the value of purchases.

		$
Opening payables		142,600
Cash paid		542,300
Discounts received		13,200
Goods returned		27,500
Closing payables		137,800

     A $302,600
     B $506,400
     C $523,200
     D $578,200

2   These figures relate to receivables:

Balance at 1/1/X1	$2,500
Balance at 31/12/X1	$2,000
Cash from receivables	$10,600
Contra with payables ledger	$5,000
Increase in allowance for receivables	$580

What were sales during the year?

     A $5,100
     B $14,520
     C $15,100
     D $15,680

3   An employee has a gross monthly salary of $1,000. In September the tax deducted was $200, the employee's national insurance was $60, and the employer's national insurance was $100. What was the charge for salaries in the income statement?

     A $740
     B $940
     C $1,000
     D $1,100

4   W is registered for sales tax. The managing director has asked four staff in the accounts department why the output tax for the last quarter does not equal 17.5% of sales (17.5% is the rate of sales tax). Which one of the following four replies she received was *not* correct?

     A   The company had some exports that were not liable to sales tax
     B   The company made some sales of zero-rated products
     C   The company made some sales of exempt products
     D   The company sold some products to businesses not registered for sales tax

5   A business has opening inventory of $12,000 and closing inventory of $18,000. Purchase returns were $5,000. The cost of goods sold was $111,000.

Purchases were

A $100,000
B $110,000
C $116,000
D $122,000

6   A business commenced with capital in cash of $1,000. Inventory costing $800 is purchased on credit, and half is sold for $1,000 plus sales tax, the customer paying in cash at once. The sales tax rate is 17½%.

The accounting equation after these transactions would show:

A   Assets $1,775 less Liabilities $175 equals Capital $1,600
B   Assets $2,175 less Liabilities $975 equals Capital $1,200
C   Assets $2,575 less Liabilities $800 equals Capital $1,775
D   Assets $2,575 less Liabilities $975 equals Capital $1,600

7   A purchase invoice shows 10 items priced at $120 less trade discount 20%. A cash discount of 2½% is allowed if settlement is made within the allowed credit period. How much will be paid if the cash discount applies?

A $1,170
B $1,200
C $936
D $960

8   Discounts received $800 were treated as discounts allowed when a traders' income statement was prepared. Therefore?

A   Profits were understated by $800
B   Profits were overstated by $800
C   Profits were understated by $1,600
D   Profits were overstated by $1,600

9   What is the correct treatment of discounts allowed and discounts received?

	Discounts allowed	Discounts Received
A	Debit payables control	Credit receivables control
B	Credit payables control	Credit receivables control
C	Debit receivables control	Credit payables control
D	Credit receivables control	Debit payables control

10   Trade receivables and payables in the final accounts of a sales tax registered trader will appear as described by which of the following?

   A   Inclusive of sales tax in the statement of financial position.

   B   Exclusive of sales tax in the statement of financial position.

   C   The sales tax is deducted and added to the sales tax a/c in the statement of financial position.

   D   Sales tax does not appear in the statement of financial position because the business simply acts as a collector on behalf of the tax authorities.

14 Control accounts, sales tax and payroll II

1   Net wages paid are?

   A   Debited to I/S as the total employment cost
   B   Debited to wages control a/c
   C   Debited to bank a/c
   D   Credited to wages control a/c

2   You are given the following information:

   Receivables at 1 January 20X3 $10,000
   Receivables at 31 December 20X3 $9,000
   Total receipts during 20X3 (including cash sales of $5,000) $85,000

   Sales on credit during 20X3 amount to

   A $81,000
   B $86,000
   C $79,000
   D $84,000

3   A supplier sends you a statement showing a balance outstanding of $14,350. Your own records show a balance outstanding of $14,500.

   The reason for this difference could be that

   A   The supplier sent an invoice for $150 which you have not yet received
   B   The supplier has allowed you $150 cash discount which you had omitted to enter in your ledgers
   C   You have paid the supplier $150 which he has not yet accounted for
   D   You have returned goods worth $150 which the supplier has not yet accounted for

4   The receivables control account at 1 May had balances of $32,750 debit and $1,275 credit. During May, sales of $125,000 were made on credit. Receipts from receivables amounted to $122,500 and cash discounts of $550 were allowed. Refunds of $1,300 were made to customers. The closing balances at 31 May could be

   A $35,175 debit and $3,000 credit
   B $35,675 debit and $2,500 credit
   C $36,725 debit and $2,000 credit
   D $36,725 debit and $1,000 credit

5   The debit side of a trial balance totals $50 more than the credit side. This could be due to

   A   A purchase of goods for $50 being omitted from the payable's account
   B   A sale of goods for $50 being omitted from the receivable's account
   C   An invoice of $25 for electricity being credited to the electricity account
   D   A receipt for $50 from a receivable being omitted from the cash book

6   A receivables control account had a closing balance of $8,500. It contained a contra to the payables control account of $400, but this had been entered on the wrong side of the control account.

   The correct balance on the control account should be

   A $7,700 debit
   B $8,100 debit
   C $8,400 debit
   D $8,900 debit

7   A trader who is not registered for sales tax purposes buys goods on credit. These goods have a list price of $2,000, exclusive of sales tax, and the trader is given a trade discount of 20%. The goods carry sales tax at 17.5%.

   The correct ledger entries to record this purchase are to debit the purchases account and to credit the supplier's account with

   A $1,600
   B $1,880
   C $2,000
   D $2,350

8   Your payables control account has a balance at 1 October 20X8 of $34,500 credit. During October, credit purchases were $78,400, cash purchases were $2,400 and payments made to suppliers, excluding cash purchases, and after deducting cash discounts of $1,200, were $68,900. Purchase returns were $4,700.

   The closing balance was:

   A $38,100
   B $40,500
   C $47,500
   D $49,900

9   The sales account is

    A   Credited with the total of sales made, including sales tax
    B   Credited with the total of sales made, excluding sales tax
    C   Debited with the total of sales made, including sales tax
    D   Debited with the total of sales made, excluding sales tax

10   At the end of the month, an organisation needs to accrue for one week's wages. The gross wages amount to $500, tax amounts to $100, employer's national insurance is $50, employees' national insurance is $40, and employees' contributions to pension scheme amount to $30. The ledger entries to record this accrual would be

A	Debit wages expense	$500	Credit national insurance payable	$90
			Credit income tax payable	$100
			Credit pension scheme payable	$30
			Credit wages accrued	$280
B	Debit wages expense	$550	Credit national insurance payable	$90
			Credit income tax payable	$100
			Credit pension scheme payable	$30
			Credit wages accrued	$330
C	Debit wages expense	$280	Credit wages accrued	$500
	Debit national insurance expense	$90		
	Debit income tax expense	$100		
	Debit pension scheme expense	$30		
D	Debit wages expense	$330	Credit wages accrued	$550
	Debit national insurance expense	$90		
	Debit income tax expense	$100		
	Debit pension scheme expense	$30		

15 Control accounts, sales tax and payroll III

1   If sales (including sales tax) amounted to $27,612.50, and purchases (excluding sales tax) amounted to $18,000, the balance on the sales tax account, assuming all items are subject to sales tax at 17.5%, would be

    A $962.50 debit
    B $962.50 credit
    C $1,682.10 debit
    D $1,682.10 credit

2   Which of the following is *not* the purpose of a receivables control account?

    A   A receivables control account provides a check on the arithmetical accuracy of the personal ledger
    B   A receivables control account helps to locate errors in the trial balance
    C   A receivables control account ensures that there are no errors in the personal ledger
    D   Control accounts deter fraud

3   The total of the balances in the payables control account is $1,500 more than the total of the payable balances extracted from the purchase ledger. Which of the following would explain this difference?

A   The purchase day book is over added by $1,500.

B   Discounts received have not been posted in the purchase ledger accounts.

C   Cash paid to payables has not been posted in some accounts in the purchase ledger.

D   A contra entry between the purchase and sales ledgers has been omitted from the purchase ledger but was posted in the control account.

4   When reconciling the list of receivables to the receivables control account, it is discovered that:

(i)   A credit balance of $150 on a customer's account has been treated as a debit balance.
(ii)   A debit balance of $120 on a customer's account has been omitted.

What is the required adjustment to the list of balances?
A   Add $30
B   Subtract $30
C   Add $180
D   Subtract $180

5   When reconciling the receivables control account to the list of balances, it was discovered that the sales daybook has been overcast by $50.

What adjustment is necessary to the list of balances?

A   No adjustment
B   Add $50
C   Subtract $50
D   Subtract $100

6   When reconciling the receivables control account to the list of balances, it is discovered that $2,000 of goods returned by customers were not recorded in the nominal ledger.

What is the required adjustment to the receivables control account?

A   Debit $2,000
B   Credit $2,000
C   Debit $4,000
D   Credit $4,000

7   When reconciling control accounts to lists of balances, a casting error in a daybook will require adjustments:

A   To both the control account and the list of balances
B   To neither the control account nor the list of balances
C   To the control account, but not the list of balances
D   To the list of balances, but not the control account

8   On 1 January 20X1, the balance on the receivables control account was $2,050.

During the year:

Sales	$90,000
Sales returns	$4,000
Cash receipts from customers	$72,800
Discounts allowed	$2,570

The cash receipts included $500 from a customer whose debt had been written off last year.

What is the balance on the receivables control account at the year-end?

A $12,680
B $13,180
C $13,680
D $17,820

9   On 1 January 20X1, the balance on the receivables control account was $2,050, by 31 December it was $5,000. Sales had been $100,000, sales returns $10,000 and cash receipts $85,500.

What was the amount settled by receivable and payable account contras?

A $1,550
B $3,100
C $3,600
D $11,550

16 Errors and suspense accounts I

1   Net profit was calculated as being $10,200. It was later discovered that capital expenditure of $3,000 had been treated as revenue expenditure, and revenue receipts of $1,400 had been treated as capital receipts.

The correct net profit should have been

A $5,800
B $8,600
C $11,800
D $14,600

2   Splodge plc's accounts contain two errors. A $10,000 bad debt written off has been deducted from sales and a $20,000 credit note received has been added to sales. Before correction, turnover was $1m and cost of sales was $800,000. What is the gross profit margin after correction of these errors?

A   17.8%
B   18.8%
C   21.2%
D   22.2%

3   After calculating your company's profit for 20X3, you discover that:

   (a)   A non-current asset costing $50,000 has been included in the purchases account;

   (b)   Stationery costing $10,000 has been included as closing inventory of raw materials, instead of inventory of stationery.

   These two errors have had the effect of

   A   Understating gross profit by $40,000 and understating net profit by $50,000
   B   Understating both gross profit and net profit by $40,000
   C   Understating gross profit by $60,000 and understating net profit by $50,000
   D   Overstating both gross profit and net profit by $60,000

4   The suspense account shows a debit balance of $100. This could be due to

   A   Entering $50 received from A Turner on the debit side of A Turner's account
   B   Entering $50 received from A Turner on the credit side of A Turner's account
   C   Undercasting the sales day book by $100
   D   Undercasting the purchases account by $100

5   You are the accountant of ABC and have extracted a trial balance at 31 October 20X4. The sum of the debit column of the trial balance exceeds the sum of the credit column by $829. A suspense account has been opened to record the difference. After preliminary investigations failed to locate any errors, you have decided to prepare draft final accounts in accordance with the prudence concept.

   The suspense account balance would be treated as

   A   An expense in the income statement
   B   Additional income in the income statement
   C   An asset in the statement of financial position
   D   A liability in the statement of financial position

6   Where a transaction is credited to the correct ledger account, but debited incorrectly to the repairs and renewals account instead of to the plant and machinery account, the error is known as an error of

   A   Omission
   B   Commission
   C   Principle
   D   Original entry

7   If a purchase return of $48 has been wrongly posted to the debit of the sales returns account, but has been correctly entered in the supplier's account, the total of the trial balance would show

   A   The credit side to be $48 more than the debit side
   B   The debit side to be $48 more than the credit side
   C   The credit side to be $96 more than the debit side
   D   The debit side to be $96 more than the credit side

8   A suspense account shows a credit balance of $130. This could be due to

A   Omitting a sale of $130 from the sales ledger

B   Recording a purchase of $130 twice in the purchases account

C   Failing to write off a bad debt of $130

D   Recording an electricity bill paid of $65 by debiting the bank account and crediting the electricity account.

9   An organisation restores its petty cash balance to $500 at the end of each month. During January, the total column in the petty cash book was recorded as being $420, and hence the imprest was restored by this amount. The analysis columns, which had been posted to the nominal ledger, totalled only $400. This error would result in

A   No imbalance in the trial balance
B   The trial balance being $20 higher on the debit side
C   The trial balance being $20 higher on the credit side
D   The petty cash balance being $20 lower than it should be

10   An invoice from a supplier of office equipment has been debited to the stationery account. This error is known as

A   An error of commission
B   An error of original entry
C   A compensating error
D   An error of principle

17 Errors and suspense accounts II

1   Which of these statements are correct?

(i)   A casting error in a day-book will stop the trial balance balancing.
(ii)   A transposition error in a daybook will stop the trial balance balancing.

A   (i) only
B   (i) and (ii)
C   (ii) only
D   Neither (i) or (ii)

2   Carriage inwards $5,000 has been recorded in the I/S account as an expense, as a result?

A   Net profit is understated by $15,000
B   Gross profit is overstated by $15,000, net profit is unchanged
C   Gross profit is understated by $15,000
D   Net profit is overstated by $15,000

3   A trial balance has failed to agree. The totals of the debits amounted to $157,800, the credit balances totalled $155,300. The difference was posted to a suspense account. Which of the following would explain this difference?

    A   Rents were recorded as

Dr	Bank	$2,500
Cr	Rents	$2,500

    B   An invoice for advertising costs $1,125 debited to advertising a/c and also debited to bank a/c

    C   An invoice for the purchase of inventory was omitted from the accounts

    D   A sundry receipt $1,125 was debited to income and credited to cash

---

4   When a trial balance was prepared, two ledger accounts were omitted:

Discounts received	$2,050
Discounts allowed	$2,500

To make a trial balance balance, a suspense account was opened.

What was the balance on the suspense account?

    A   Debit $450
    B   Credit $450
    C   Debit $4,550
    D   Credit $4,550

---

5   When a trial balance was prepared, a suspense account was opened. It was discovered that the only error that had been made was to record $2,050 of discounts received on the wrong side of the trial balance.

What is the journal to correct this error?

    A   Dr discounts received $2,050   Cr suspense $2,050
    B   Dr suspense $2,050   Cr discounts received $2,050
    C   Dr discounts received $4,100   Cr suspense $4,100
    D   Dr suspense $4,100   Cr discounts received $4,100

---

6   When a trial balance was prepared, a suspense account was opened. The only error that has been made was that when $400 written off the previous year was recovered, the bookkeeper credited the bad debts expense account and the receivables control account and debited cash.

Which journal is required to correct this error?

    A   Dr suspense $400   —   Cr receivables control $400
    B   Dr receivables control $400   Cr suspense $400
    C   Dr suspense $800   Cr receivables control $800
    D   Dr receivables control $800   Cr suspense $800

7 An error of principle would occur if

   A   Plant and machinery purchased was credited to a non-current assets account
   B   Plant and machinery purchased was debited to the purchases account
   C   Plant and machinery purchased was debited to the equipment account
   D   Plant and machinery purchased was debited to the correct account but with the wrong amount

---

8 A suspense account was opened when a trial balance failed to agree. The following errors were later discovered.

- A gas bill of $420 had been recorded in the gas account as $240
- A discount of $50 given to a customer had been credited to discounts received
- Interest received of $70 had been entered in the bank account only

The original balance on the suspense account was

   A   Debit $210
   B   Credit $210
   C   Debit $160
   D   Credit $160

---

9 An error of commission is one where

   A   A transaction has not been recorded

   B   One side of a transaction has been recorded in the wrong class of account, such as non-current assets posted to inventory

   C   An error has been made in posting a transaction

   D   The digits in a number are recorded the wrong way round

---

10 Where a transaction is entered into the correct ledger accounts, but the wrong amount is used, the error is known as an error of

   A   Omission
   B   Original entry
   C   Commission
   D   Principle

---

18 Errors and suspense accounts III

1 Which ONE of the following is an error of principle?

   A A gas bill credited to the gas account and debited to the bank account

   B The purchase of a non-current asset credited to the asset account at cost and debited to the payable's account

   C The purchase of a non-current asset debited to the purchases account and credited to the payable's account

   D The payment of wages debited and credited to the correct accounts, but using the wrong amount

2 When a trial balance was prepared, the closing inventory of $20,400 was omitted. To make the trial balance balance, a suspense account was opened.

   What was the balance on the suspense account?

   A Nil
   B Debit $20,400
   C Credit $20,400
   D Debit $40,800

3 When a trial balance was prepared, opening inventory of $1,000 was omitted. To make the trial balance balance, a suspense account was opened.

   What was the balance on the suspense account?

   A Nil
   B Debit $1,000
   C Credit $1,000
   D Debit $2,000

4 Some inventory taken by the owner of a business has not yet been recorded. When this transaction is recorded:

   A Profit will rise and net assets fall
   B Profit will rise and net assets stay the same
   C Profit will fall and net assets rise
   D Profit will fall and net assets stay the same

5 Materials used to improve some machinery have been treated as purchases in the draft accounts. The necessary correction will:

   A Increase both profit and net assets
   B Increase profit and reduce net assets
   C Reduce profit and increase net assets
   D Reduce both profit and net assets

6   A loan repayable in 16 months has been included in current liabilities in the draft statement of financial position.

The necessary adjustment will:

A   Increase both current assets and net assets
B   Increase current assets and reduce net assets
C   Reduce current assets and increase net assets
D   Increase net current assets but leave net assets unchanged

7   It is realised that inventory which cost $5,000 with a net realisable value of $6,000 was excluded from a inventory take. The correction of this omission causes profit to

A   Fall by $1,000
B   Rise by $1,000
C   Fall by $5,000
D   Rise by $5,000

19 Sole trader's accounts

1   An increase in inventory of $250, a decrease in the bank balance of $400 and an increase in payables of $1,200 result in

A   A decrease in working capital of $1,350
B   An increase in working capital of $1,350
C   A decrease in working capital of $1,050
D   An increase in working capital of $1,050

2   A business has the following items extracted from its accounting records. Sales $150,000, opening inventory $10,000, closing inventory $15,000. The business applies a constant mark up of 25%. Calculate the total purchases for the year.

A $115,000
B $145,000
C $117,500
D $125,000

3   The capital of a sole trader would change as a result of

A   A payable being paid his account by cheque
B   Raw materials being purchased on credit
C   Non-current assets being purchased on credit
D   Wages being paid in cash

4 An organisation's year end is 30 September. On 1 January 20X6 the organisation took out a loan of $100,000 with annual interest of 12%. The interest is payable in equal instalments on the first day of April, July, October and January in arrears.

How much should be charged to the income statement for the year ended 30 September 20X6, and how much should be accrued on the statement of financial position?

	Income statement	SOFP
A	$12,000	$3,000
B	$9,000	$3,000
C	$9,000	nil
D	$6,000	$3,000

5 A business's bank balance increased by $750,000 during its last financial year. During the same period it issued shares of $1 million and repaid a debenture of $750,000. It purchased non-current assets for $200,000 and charged depreciation of $100,000. Working capital (other than the bank balance) increased by $575,000.

Its profit for the year was

A $1,175,000
B $1,275,000
C $1,325,000
D $1,375,000

6 A sole trader's business made a profit of $32,500 during the year ended 31 March 20X8. This figure was after deducting $100 per week wages for himself. In addition, he put his home telephone bill through the business books, amounting to $400 plus sales tax at 17.5%. He is registered for sales tax and therefore has charged only the net amount to his income statement.

His capital at 1 April 20X7 was $6,500. His capital at 31 March 20X8 was

A $33,730
B $33,800
C $38,930
D $39,000

7 A business can make a profit and yet have a reduction in its bank balance. Which ONE of the following might cause this to happen?

A The sales of non-current assets at a loss
B The charging of depreciation in the income statement
C The lengthening of the period of credit given to customers
D The lengthening of the period of credit taken from suppliers

8   The purpose of charging depreciation on non-current assets is to

    A   Put money aside to replace the assets when required
    B   Show the assets in the statement of financial position at their current market value
    C   Ensure that the profit is not understated
    D   Spread the net cost of the assets over their estimated useful life

9   Hengist, a sole trader, has calculated that his cost of sales for the year is $144,000. His sales figure for the year includes an amount of $2,016 being the amount paid by Hengist himself into the business bank account for goods withdrawn for private use. The figure of $2,016 was calculated by adding a mark-up of 12% to the cost of the goods. His gross profit percentage on all other goods sold was 20%.

What is the total sales figure for the year?

    A $172,656
    B $177,750
    C $179,766
    D $180,000

10   At 31 December 20X1, a business had:

Motor cars	2,000
Inventory	500
Receivables	300
Accrued Electricity Expense	50
Rent prepaid	200

At 31 December 20X2, it had:

Motor cars	2,500
Inventory	100
Receivables	50
Payables	600
Accrued Electricity Expense	100
Rent prepaid	250

The owner has drawn $1,000 in cash over the year.

What is the profit or loss?

    A   Loss $250
    B   Profit $250
    C   Loss $750
    D   Profit $750

11   In a statement of financial position, capital plus profit less drawings must always equal:

    A   Non-current assets
    B   Current assets
    C   Net current assets
    D   Net assets

12 A sole trader decides to 'net off' the amount he owes to a supplier who is also a customer.

Which of these statements is wrong?

A   Net assets will not change
B   Non-current assets will not change
C   Net current assets will not change
D   Current assets will not change

13 Which statement is wrong for a statement of financial position to balance?

A   Net assets = Proprietor's fund
B   Net assets = Capital + profit + drawings
C   Net assets = Capital + profit – drawings
D   Non-current assets + net current assets = capital + profit – drawings

20 Limited liability companies I

1   A company has an authorised share capital of 1,000,000 ordinary shares of $1 each, of which 800,000 have
been issued at a premium of 50c each, thereby raising capital of $1,200,000. The directors are considering
allocating $120,000 for dividend payments this year.

This amounts to a dividend of

A   12c per share
B   10c per share
C   15c per share
D   12%

2   Which one of the following would you expect to find in the SOCIE of a limited company, for the current year?

A   Preference dividend proposed during the previous year, but paid in the current year
B   Preference dividend proposed during the current year, but paid in the following year
C   Directors' fees
D   Auditors' fees

3   Revenue reserves are

A   Accumulated and undistributed profits of a company
B   Amounts which cannot be distributed as dividends
C   Amounts set aside out of profits to replace revenue items
D   Amounts set aside out of profits for a specific purpose

4 A company has $100,000 of ordinary shares at a par value of 10 cents each and 100,000 5% preference shares at a par value of 50 cents each. The directors decide to declare a dividend of 5 cents per ordinary share.

The total amount (ignoring tax) to be paid out in dividends amounts to

A $5,000
B $7,500
C $52,500
D $55,000

5 The correct ledger entries needed to record the issue of 200,000 $1 shares at a premium of 30p, and paid for by cheque, in full, would be

A	DEBIT	share capital account	$200,000
	CREDIT	share premium account	$60,000
	CREDIT	bank account	$140,000
B	DEBIT	bank account	$260,000
	CREDIT	share capital account	$200,000
	CREDIT	share premium account	$60,000
C	DEBIT	share capital account	$200,000
	CREDIT	share premium account	$60,000
	CREDIT	bank account	$260,000
D	DEBIT	bank account	$200,000
	DEBIT	share premium account	$60,000
	CREDIT	share capital account	$260,000

6 A particular source of finance has the following characteristics: a fixed return, a fixed repayment date, it is secured and the return is classified as an expense.

Is the source of finance

A Ordinary share
B Hire purchase
C Loan stock
D Preference share

7 Which of the following items does not appear under the heading 'reserves' on a company statement of financial position?

A Share premium account
B Retained profits
C Revaluation surpluses
D Proposed dividends

8   Which of the following statements regarding a company income statement is correct?

    A   The Companies Act 1985 defines the expenses which are reported under 'cost of sales'.

    B   'Depreciation' appears as a separate heading.

    C   Interest payable is deducted from profit after taxation.

    D   Bad debts will be included under one of the statutory expense headings (usually administrative expenses).

9   A company has $500,000, 15% debentures which were originally issued at par. The company had paid interest half yearly but the final instalment is outstanding at the year end. Which of the following statements is correct?

    A   The interest charge in the income statement account will be $75,000

    B   The interest charge in the income statement account will be $37,500

    C   The statement of financial position will contain a liability for outstanding interest of $75,000

    D   The interest charge in the income statement account will be $112,500

10   A company has authorised capital of 50,000 5% preference shares of $2 each and 500,000 ordinary shares with a par value of 20c each. All of the preference shares have been issued, and 400,000 ordinary shares have been issued at a premium of 30c each. Interim dividends of 5c per ordinary share plus half the preference dividend have been paid during the current year. A final dividend of 15c per ordinary share is declared.

The total of dividends payable for the year is

    A $82,500

    B $85,000

    C $102,500

    D $105,000

21 Limited liability companies II

1   The record of how the profit or loss of a company has been allocated to distributions and reserves is found in the

    A   Capital account

    B   Income statement

    C   Reserves account

    D   Statement of changes in equity

2   A company had dividends payable of $35,000 at 31 December 20X1 and dividends payable of $45,000 at 31 December 20X2. The dividends in the income statement for the year to 31 December 20X2 were $60,000.

What would appear in the cashflow statement for 'dividends paid'?

A $10,000
B $50,000
C $60,000
D $70,000

---

3   In a set of company accounts, which would normally increase administration expenses?

A   Reduction in the allowance for receivables
B   Depreciation of machinery in the factory
C   Payment of the audit fee
D   Payment of production director's salary

---

4   Revenue reserves would decrease if a company

A   Sets aside profits to pay future dividends
B   Transfers amounts into 'general reserves'
C   Issues shares at a premium
D   Pays dividends

---

5   Which ONE of the following does NOT form part of the equity capital of a limited company?

A   Preference share capital
B   Share premium
C   Revaluation reserve
D   Ordinary share capital

---

22 Incomplete records

1   The bookkeeper of Leggit has disappeared. There is no cash in the till and theft is suspected. It is known that the cash balance at the beginning of the year was $240. Since then, total sales have amounted to $41,250. Credit customers owed $2,100 at the beginning of the year and owe $875 now. Cheques banked from credit customers have totalled $24,290. Expenses paid from the till receipts amount to $1,850 and cash receipts of $9,300 have been lodged in the bank.

How much has the bookkeeper stolen during the period?

A $7,275
B $9,125
C $12,155
D $16,575

2   A business achieves a margin of 25% on sales. Opening inventory was $18,000, closing inventory was $28,000 and purchases totalled $300,000. Calculate the sales for the period.

    A $386,666
    B $362,500
    C $413,230
    D $400,000

3   A business has opening inventory $15,000, achieves a mark up of 25% on sales, sales totalled $500,000, purchases were $420,000. Calculate closing inventory.

    A $15,000
    B $20,000
    C $60,000
    D $35,000

4   A business sells goods earning a constant 25% mark up. Sales in period amounted to $500,000. Opening inventory was $10,000, closing inventory is valued at $20,000. Purchases were $450,000. The owner suspects theft, calculate the amount of the inventory losses.

    A $40,000
    B $65,000
    C $60,000
    D $50,000

5   A company achieves a gross profit (margin) of 20% on sales. Opening inventory was $5,000, payables at the start of the period were $4,000. Sales in the period amounted to $50,000. Year end payables were $6,000 and the business had paid payables $37,000. All the inventory had been stolen at the end of the period, what was it's value?

    A $nil
    B $2,000
    C $6,500
    D $4,000

6   A business commenced with a bank balance of $3,250; it subsequently purchased goods on credit for $10,000; gross profit mark-up was 120%; half the goods were sold for cash, less cash discount of 5%; all takings were banked.

    The resulting net profit was

    A $700
    B $3,700
    C $5,450
    D $5,700

7   An organisation's cash book has an opening balance in the bank column of $485 credit. The following
     transactions then took place.

     (i)   Cash sales $1,450 including sales tax of $150
     (ii)   Receipts from customers of debts of $2,400
     (iii) Payments to payables of debts of $1,800 less 5% cash discount
     (iv)   Dishonoured cheques from customers amounting to $250

     The resulting balance in the bank column of the cash book should be

     A $1,255 debit
     B $1,405 debit
     C $1,905 credit
     D $2,375 credit

8   During the year, all sales were made at a gross profit margin of 15%. Sales were $25,500, purchases were
     $22,000 and closing inventory was $4,000.

     What was opening inventory?

     A $3,675
     B $4,000
     C $4,174
     D $4,325

9   During the year, all sales were made with a 20% mark-up on cost. Sales were $25,500, purchases were
     $26,000 and closing inventory was $10,000.

     What was opening inventory?

     A $4,150
     B $5,250
     C $10,000
     D $14,750

10   At 1/1/X1 receivables owed $3,050, at 31/12/X1 they owed $4,000. Cash received from receivables during
     the year was $22,000 (including $1,000 bad debt recovered). All sales were made at a 20% gross profit
     margin and no inventory are held.

     What were purchases for the year?

     A $21,950
     B $18,292
     C $17,560
     D $4,390

11   If the mark-up is 30% and the cost of sales is $28,000, and expenses are $14,000, what is the net profit?

    A   Profit $2,000
    B   Loss $2,000
    C   Profit $5,600
    D   Loss $5,600

12   If sales were $25,500, and cost of sales was $21,250, what was the gross profit percentage?

    A   16.67%
    B   20%
    C   83.333%
    D   120%

13   A sole trader has net assets of $19,000 at 30 April 20X0. During the year to 30 April 20X0, he introduced $9,800 additional capital into the business. Profits were $8,000, of which he withdrew $4,200. His capital at 1 May 20W9 was:

    A $3,000
    B $5,400
    C $13,000
    D $16,600

23 Income and expenditure accounts

1   A club takes credit for subscriptions when they become due. On 1 January 20X5 arrears of subscriptions amounted to $38 and subscriptions paid in advance were $72. On 31 December 20X5 the amounts were $48 and $80 respectively. Subscription receipts during the year were $790.

In the income and expenditure account for 20X5 the income from subscriptions would be shown as:

    A $748
    B $788
    C $790
    D $792

2   A club takes no credit for subscriptions due until they are received. On 1 January 20X5 arrears of subscriptions amounted to $24 and subscriptions paid in advance were $14. On 31 December 20X5 the amounts were $42 and $58 respectively. Subscription receipts during the year were $1,024.

In the income and expenditure account for 20X5 the income from subscriptions would be shown as:

    A $956
    B $980
    C $998
    D $1,050

3   For many years, life membership of the Tipton Poetry Association cost $100, but with effect from 1 January 20X5 the rate has been increased to $120. The balance on the life membership fund at 31 December 20X4 was $3,780 and membership details at that date were as follows:

	No of members
Joined more than 19 years ago	32
Joined within the last 19 years	64
	96

The Association's accounting policy is to release life subscriptions to income over a period of 20 years beginning with the year of enrolment.

During 20X5, four new members were enrolled and one other member (who had joined in 20X1) died.

What is the balance on the life membership fund at 31 December 20X5?

A $3,591
B $3,841
C $3,916
D $4,047

4   A debit balance on an income and expenditure account prepared for a club is dealt with by?

A   Deduction from the club accumulated fund
B   Addition to the bank balance in the statement of financial position
C   Addition to the club accumulated fund
D   Inclusion in the statement of financial position as a prepayment

5   A club has 200 members, each should pay $20 for subscriptions. At the start of the year 20 members owed subscriptions, at the end of the year 5 members had prepaid subscriptions. 3 members subscriptions were unpaid and written off as uncollectable during the year. Calculate the cash receipts for the year. (Assume the annual subscription remains at $20.)

A $3,640
B $4,240
C $4,560
D $4,440

6   Calculate the subscription income for the XYZ Social Club using the following data. Arrears 1.1.20X1 $700, prepaid in advance 1.1.20X1 $1,500, arrears 31.12.20X1 $1,200, paid in advance 31.12.20X1 $3,200, cash received from members $14,200.

A $13,000
B $14,200
C $11,400
D $17,000

BPP)))
LEARNING MEDIA

7　Which of the following is the correct accounting treatment of life membership subscriptions paid in advance by members for an indefinite period?

    A   Credit to revenue in full in the year of receipt
    B   Carry as an asset on the statement of financial position
    C   Credit to revenue from a life membership fund over a defined period in accordance with club policy
    D   Add to the accumulated fund of the club

8　In a not-for-profit organisation, the accumulated fund is

    A   Long-term liabilities plus current liabilities plus current assets
    B   Non-current assets less current liabilities less long-term liabilities
    C   The balance on the general reserves account
    D   Non-current assets plus net current assets less long-term liabilities

9　An income and expenditure account is

    A   A summary of the cash and bank transactions for a period
    B   Another name for a receipts and payments account
    C   Similar to a income statement in reflecting revenue earned and expenses incurred during a period
    D   A statement of financial position as prepared for a non-profit making organisation

10　A club received subscriptions during 20X5 totalling $12,500. Of these, $800 related to 20X4 and $400 related to 20X6. There were subscriptions in arrears at the end of 20X5 of $250. The subscriptions to be included in the income and expenditure account for 20X5 amount to

    A $11,050
    B $11,550
    C $11,850
    D $12,350

11　Life membership fees payable to a club are usually dealt with by

    A   Crediting the total received to a life membership fees account and transferring a proportion each year to the income and expenditure account

    B   Crediting the total received to the income and expenditure account in the year in which these fees are received

    C   Debiting the total received to a life membership fees account and transferring a proportion each year to the income and expenditure account

    D   Debiting the total received to the income and expenditure account in the year in which these fees are received

12 A club's membership fees account shows a debit balance of $150 and a credit balance of $90 at 1 June 20X7. During the year ending 31 May 20X8, subscriptions received amounted to $4,750. Subscriptions overdue from the year ended 31 May 20X7, of $40, are to be written off. At 31 May 20X8, subscriptions paid in advance amount to $75.

The amount to be transferred to the income and expenditure account for the year ending 31 May 20X8 is

A $4,575
B $4,655
C $4,775
D $4,875

13 The difference between a receipts and payments account and an income and expenditure account is:

A   A receipts and payments account is prepared on an accruals basis and an income and expenditure account on a cash basis.

B   A receipts and payments account is prepared on a cash basis and an income and expenditure account on an accruals basis.

C   A receipts and payments account is prepared for a not for profit organisation and an income and expenditure account for a business.

D   A receipts and payments account for a manufacturing business and an income and expenditure account for a non-manufacturing business.

14 Which of these statements are true about the difference between a income statement and a receipts and payments account?

(i)   A income statement is prepared for a business and a receipts and payments account for a not-for-profit organisation.

(ii) A income statement is prepared for a manufacturing business and a receipts and payments account for a non-manufacturing business.

A   Both true
B   Both false
C   (i) true, (ii) false
D   (i) false, (ii) true

15 A receipts and payments account is similar to:

A   An income and expenditure account
B   A income statement
C   A trading account
D   A cash book summary

16 The subscriptions receivable account of a club commenced the year with subscriptions in arrears of $50 and subscriptions in advance of $75. During the year, $12,450 was received in subscriptions, including all of the arrears and $120 for next year's subscriptions

The amount to be taken to the income and expenditure account for the year is

A $12,205
B $12,355
C $12,545
D $12,595

24 Manufacturing accounts

1   Your company sells goods on 29 December 20X3, on sale or return; the final date for return or payment in full is 10 January 20X4. The costs of manufacturing the product are all incurred and paid for in 20X3 except for an outstanding bill for carriage outwards which is still unpaid.

The associated revenues and expenses of the transaction should be dealt with in the income statement by

A   Including all revenues and all expenses in 20X3
B   Including all revenues and all expenses in 20X4
C   Including expenses in 20X3 and revenues in 20X4
D   Including the revenue and the carriage outwards in 20X4, and the other expenses in 20X3

2   The following information relates to a company at its year end.

	$
Inventory at beginning of year	
Raw materials	10,000
Work-in-progress	2,000
Finished goods	34,000
Inventory at end of year	
Raw materials	11,000
Work-in-progress	4,000
Finished goods	30,000
Purchases of raw materials	50,000
Direct wages	40,000
Royalties on goods sold	3,000
Production overheads	60,000
Distribution costs	55,000
Administration expenses	70,000
Sales	300,000

The cost of goods manufactured during the year is

A $147,000
B $151,000
C $153,000
D $154,000

3   If work-in-progress decreases during the period, then

    A   Prime cost will decrease
    B   Prime cost will increase
    C   The factory cost of goods completed will decrease
    D   The factory cost of goods completed will increase

4   A manufacturer has the following figures for the year ended 30 September 20X6:

Direct materials	$8,000
Factory overheads	$12,000
Direct labour	$10,000
Increase in work-in-progress	$4,000

Prime cost is

    A $18,000
    B $26,000
    C $30,000
    D $34,000

5   An increase in the figure for work-in-progress will

    A   Increase the prime cost
    B   Decrease the prime cost
    C   Increase the cost of goods sold
    D   Decrease the factory cost of goods completed

6   You are given the following information for the year ended 31 October 20X7:

	$
Purchases of raw materials	112,000
Returns inwards	8,000
Decrease in inventories of raw materials	8,000
Direct wages	42,000
Carriage outwards	4,000
Carriage inwards	3,000
Production overheads	27,000
Increase in work-in-progress	10,000

The value of factory cost of goods completed is

    A $174,000
    B $182,000
    C $183,000
    D $202,000

7   Your firm has the following manufacturing figures.

	$
Prime cost	56,000
Factory overheads	4,500
Opening work in progress	6,200
Factory cost of goods completed	57,000

Closing work-in-progress is

A $700
B $2,700
C $9,700
D $11,700

8   The prime cost of goods manufactured is the total of

A   All factory costs before adjusting for work-in progress
B   All factory costs of goods completed
C   All materials and labour
D   Direct factory costs

25 Audit I

1   A 'true and fair view' is one which

A   Presents the accounts in such a way as to exclude errors which would affect the actions of those reading them

B   Occurs when the accounts have been audited

C   Shows the accounts of an organisation in an understandable format

D   Shows the assets on the statement of financial position at their current market price

2   Your company auditor insists that it is necessary to record items of plant separately and to depreciate them over several years, but that items of office equipment, such as hand-held stapling machines, can be grouped together and written off against profits immediately.

The main reason for this difference in treatment between the two items is because

A   Treatment of the two items must be consistent with treatment in previous periods

B   Items of plant last for several years, whereas hand-held stapling machines last only for months

C   Hand-held stapling machines are not regarded as material items

D   Items of plant are revalued from time to time, whereas hand-held stapling machines are recorded at historical cost

3   The main purpose of an audit is to

    A   Detect errors and fraud
    B   Ensure that the accounts are accurate
    C   Determine that the accounts show a true and fair view of the financial state of the organisation
    D   Carry out compliance tests on the internal control system

4   The responsibility for ensuring that all accounting transactions are properly recorded and summarised in the final accounts lies with

    A   The external auditors
    B   The internal auditors
    C   The shareholders
    D   The directors

5   Which of the following statements is correct?

    A   External auditors report to the directors
    B   External auditors are appointed by the directors
    C   External auditors are required to give a report to shareholders
    D   External auditors correct errors in financial statements

6   What is an audit trail in a computerised accounting system?

    A   A list of all the transactions in a period
    B   A list of all the transactions in a ledger account in a period
    C   A list of all the items checked by the auditor
    D   A list of all the nominal ledger codes

7   Which is the following statements is *not* correct?

    A   Internal auditors review value for money
    B   Internal auditors should not liaise with external auditors
    C   Internal audit is part of internal control
    D   Internal audit should be independent of the activities it audits

8   Which of the following statements concerning the status of an external auditor is incorrect?

    A   All companies must appoint external auditors
    B   The duties of an auditor are defined by the Companies Act 2006
    C   The auditor gives an opinion on the financial statements
    D   The auditor reports to the members of the company

9   Which of the following is *not* an activity which internal auditors would normally carry out?

    A   Fraud investigations
    B   Value for money studies
    C   Systems appraisal
    D   The statutory audit

10   A major aim of the internal auditors is to

    A   Reduce the costs of the external auditors by carrying out some of their duties
    B   Support the work of the external auditors
    C   Prepare the financial accounts
    D   Report to shareholders on the accuracy of the accounts

26 Audit II

1   Ensuring that the assets of a company are properly safeguarded and utilised efficiently and effectively is part of

    A   The stewardship function exercised by the directors
    B   The external auditor's responsibility
    C   The function of the financial accountant
    D   The internal auditor's responsibility

2   A true and fair view is given by the accounts when:

    A   Assets are stated at their true values in the statement of financial position

    B   They have been audited and found to be accurate

    C   They fairly reflect the financial position of an organisation, sufficient for users of the accounts to make proper judgements

    D   The auditors are able to certify that they contain no errors or omissions, and that no fraud has been committed

3   Which is the single most important attribute of an auditor (external or internal)?

    A   Professional skills and training
    B   Good communication skills
    C   Independence
    D   Accuracy

4   Which of the following is not a key difference between internal and external auditors?

    A   Reporting responsibilities
    B   Professionalism
    C   Appointment
    D   Objectives

5   Which of the following statements concerning the authorisation of journal entries is correct?

A   All journal entries should be authorised by an appropriate person in writing

B   The limits for authorisation should be specified and all journal entries should be signed by the originating and the authorising signatories

C   There is no need to authorise low value journal entries

D   Journal entries input to a computer system are impossible to authorise

6   What does the phrase 'proper cut-off procedures' mean in relation to the sale of goods?

A   All goods are invoiced to customers.

B   Inventory records correctly record receipts and dispatches of goods for resale.

C   Arrangements to ensure that all goods dispatched prior to the cut off point are either invoiced or accrued in the financial statements.

D   Having place arrangements to check invoices prior to dispatch to customers.

7   An internal auditor identifies an internal control weakness in an accounting system. What action should now be taken?

A   Consider the effect of the weakness and identify counter controls
B   Report to management
C   Instruct the operators of the system to change the procedures in use
D   Do nothing

8   Which of the following internal control procedures will *not* help to detect fictitious employees on the payroll of a large company?

A   Identification of employees by an independent official at the distribution of wages
B   Paying employees by bank transfer
C   Ensuring that all employees have contracts of employment prepared by the personnel department
D   Ensuring that changes to the company payroll system (eg starters and leavers) are authorised

9   What do you understand by the term 'management fraud'?

A   Theft by managers
B   Fraud designed to improve the companies position or performance
C   Using creative accounting
D   Manipulating the company share price

10 The term 'audit trail' refers to?

A   The ability to trace transactions through a processing system by reference to documentation
B   The retention of documents
C   Explaining how systems work to the company's auditors
D   Designing systems so that controls operate efficiently

11   The primary reason for an external audit is to:

    A   Give an opinion on the financial statements
    B   Detect any major errors or frauds
    C   Aid decision making by management
    D   Aid decision making by shareholders

12   True and fair is determined by reference to:

    A   Compliance with company law
    B   Compliance with accounting standards
    C   Compliance with generally accepted accounting practice
    D   Compliance with previous financial statement

13   Who appoints external auditors?

    A   Directors
    B   Employees
    C   Managers
    D   Shareholders

27 Statements of cash flows

1   In the operating profit note of a statement of cash flows it is usual to find adjustments for items not involving cash movement. Which one of the following items might appear under such a heading?

    A   The profit on disposal of non-current assets
    B   The accumulated depreciation on non-current assets
    C   The income statement charge for taxation
    D   The allowance for receivables

2   Which of the following would correctly calculate the operating cash flows for a company?

    A   Operating profit plus inventory increase less receivable decrease plus payable increase
    B   Operating profit less inventory increase less receivable increase plus payable increase
    C   Operating profit less inventory increase plus receivable decrease less payable increase
    D   Operating profit less inventory increase less receivable increase less payable increase

3   A company has the following payments and receipts during its accounting period. Calculate the 'financing' cash flow figure for its statement of cash flows. Issue of shares $515,000, loan stock repaid $200,000, share premium received $230,000, proceeds of a rights issue $315,000, interest paid $115,000.

    A $860,000
    B $545,000
    C $745,000
    D $630,000

4   A company has the following non-current asset transactions. Non-current assets purchased cost
     $1,200,000, part of the costs of these ($100,000) are unpaid at the year end. Non-current assets value
     $500,000 are also leased. Non-current assets sold for $50,000. Depreciation for the period is $170,000.
     Calculate the capital investment cash flow.

     A $880,000 (outflow)
     B $1,050,000 (outflow)
     C $1,100,000 (outflow)
     D $1,150,000 (outflow)

5   A non-current asset note includes

	At 31/12/X4	At 31/12/X3
Plant and machinery		
Cost	10,500	9,400
Depreciation	3,400	4,100
Motor vehicles		
Cost	12,600	10,500
Depreciation	4,100	3,600

     Plant and machinery with a cost of $2,000 and a written down value of $1,200 was sold during the year.

     In the statement of cash flows what is the figure for payments to acquire non-current assets in the year to
     31/12/X4?
     A $3,200
     B $4,400
     C $4,700
     D $5,200

6   When comparing two statements of financial position you notice that:

     (i)   Last year the company had included in current assets investments of $10,000. This year there are no
           investments in current assets.

     (ii) Last year the company had an overdraft of $8,000, this year the overdraft is $4,000.

     In the statement of cash flows, the change in cash would be:
     A   Increase $4,000
     B   Decrease $4,000
     C   Increase $6,000
     D   Decrease $6,000

7   A company statement of financial position shows dividends payable of $50,000 at 31 December 20X2 and
     $75,000 at 31 December 20X3. The SOCIE for the year ended 31 December 20X3 shows dividends of
     $65,000. What is the figure for dividends paid to be included in the statement of cash flows?

     A $50,000
     B $75,000
     C $65,000
     D $40,000

28 Interpretation of accounts I

1   Horsa's sales follow a seasonal pattern. Monthly sales in the final quarter of the year are twice as high as during other periods. He also benefits from a higher mark-up during the final quarter: an average of 25% on cost compared with 20% during the rest of the year.

Horsa's sales in 20X9 totalled $210,000. What was the amount of his gross profit?

A $36,750
B $37,800
C $39,667
D $46,200

2   Which one of the following formulae should be used to calculate the rate of inventory turnover in a retail business?

A   Sales divided by average inventory
B   Sales divided by year-end inventory
C   Purchases divided by year-end inventory
D   Cost of sales divided by average inventory

3   A company's working capital was $43,200. Subsequently, the following transactions occurred.

(a)   Payables were paid $3,000 by cheque.
(b)   A bad debt of $250 was written off.
(c)   Inventory valued at $100 was sold for $230 on credit.

Working capital is now

A $43,080
B $46,080
C $40,080
D $42,850

4   The formula for calculating the rate of inventory turnover is

A   Average inventory at cost divided by cost of goods sold
B   Sales divided by average inventory at cost
C   Sales divided by average inventory at selling price
D   Cost of goods sold divided by average inventory at cost

5   Given a selling price of $350 and a gross profit mark-up of 40%, the cost price would be

A $100
B $140
C $210
D $250

6   Which of the following transactions would result in an increase in capital employed?

     A   Selling inventory at a profit
     B   Writing off a bad debt
     C   Paying a payable in cash
     D   Increasing the bank overdraft to purchase a non-current asset

7   Sales are $110,000. Purchases are $80,000. Opening inventory is $12,000. Closing inventory is $10,000.

     The rate of inventory turnover is

     A   7.27 times
     B   7.45 times
     C   8 times
     D   10 times

8   The rate of inventory turnover is 6 times where

     A   Sales are $120,000 and average inventory at selling price is $20,000
     B   Purchases are $240,000 and average inventory at cost is $40,000
     C   Cost of goods sold is $180,000 and average inventory at cost is $30,000
     D   Net purchases are $90,000 and closing inventory at cost is $15,000

9   Working capital will reduce by $500 if

     A   Goods costing $3,000 are sold for $3,500 on credit
     B   Goods costing $3,000 are sold for $3,500 cash
     C   Non-current assets costing $500 are purchased on credit
     D   Non-current assets with a net book value of $750 are sold for $250 cash

10   From the following information regarding the year to 31 August 20X6, what is the payables' payment period?

	$
Sales	43,000
Cost of sales	32,500
Opening inventory	6,000
Closing inventory	3,800
Payables at 31 August 20X6	4,750

     A   40 days
     B   50 days
     C   53 days
     D   57 days

29 Interpretation of accounts II

1   The draft statement of financial position of B at 31 March 20X8 is set out below.

		$	$
Non-current assets			450
Current assets:	Inventory	65	
	Receivables	110	
	Prepayments	30	
		205	
Current liabilities	Payables	30	
	Bank overdraft (Note)	50	
		80	
			125
			575
Long-term liability: Loan			(75)
			500
Ordinary share capital			400
Income statement			100
			500

Note. The bank overdraft first occurred on 30 September 20X7.

What is the gearing of the company?

A   13%
B   16%
C   20%
D   24%

2   Which of the following is not a ratio which is used to explain how well the operations of a business have been managed?

A   Asset turnover
B   Profit margin
C   Gearing
D   Return on capital employed

3   An increase in selling prices may lead to which of the following effects?

A   Asset turnover will increase
B   Profit margins will fall
C   Profit margins may increase subject to a fall in asset turnover
D   Return on capital employed will increase

4   Working capital is?

      A   Non-current assets + net current assets
      B   Current assets – current liabilities
      C   Total assets – total liabilities
      D   Liquid current assets – current liabilities

5   A firm buys materials on 2 months credit, they spend 2 months in inventory and 0.5 months in production. Finished goods are normally retained for 3 months before sale and on average receivables take 3 months to pay. Calculate the time taken for cash to cycle through the business.

      A   6.5 months
      B   8.5 months
      C   3.5 months
      D   2.5 months

6   Arrange the following current assets in order of increasing liquidity (least to most liquid).

      (A)   Inventory
      (B)   Cash
      (C)   Receivables
      (D)   Prepayments

      A   B, D, C, A
      B   A, B, C, D
      C   A, C, D, B
      D   D, B, C, A

30 Ratios I

1   A business operates on a gross profit margin of $33^1/_3\%$. Gross profit on a sale was $800, and expenses were $680.

      The net profit percentage is

      A   3.75%
      B   5%
      C   11.25%
      D   22.67%

2   During the year ended 31 October 20X7, your organisation made a gross profit of $60,000, which represented a mark-up of 50%. Opening inventory was $12,000 and closing inventory was $18,000.

      The rate of inventory turnover was

      A   4 times
      B   6.7 times
      C   7.3 times
      D   8 times

3   A business has the following trading account for the year ending 31 May 20X8:

	$	$
Sales turnover		45,000
Opening inventory	4,000	
Purchases	26,500	
	30,500	
Less: closing inventory	6,000	
		24,500
Gross profit		20,500

Its rate of inventory turnover for the year is

A   4.9 times
B   5.3 times
C   7.5 times
D   9 times

4   A company's gearing ratio would rise if

A   A decrease in long-term loans is *less* than a decrease in shareholders' funds
B   A decrease in long-term loan is *more* than a decrease in shareholders' funds
C   Interest rates rose
D   Dividends were paid

5   A company has the following details extracted from its statement of financial position:

	$'000
Inventorys	1,900
Receivables	1,000
Bank overdraft	100
Payables	1,000

Its liquidity position could be said to be

A   Very well-controlled because its current assets far outweigh its current liabilities
B   Poorly-controlled because its quick assets are less than its current liabilities
C   Poorly-controlled because its current ratio is significantly higher than the industry norm of 1.8
D   Poorly-controlled because it has a bank overdraft

6   The gross profit mark-up is 40% where

A   Sales are $120,000 and gross profit is $48,000
B   Sales are $120,000 and cost of sales is $72,000
C   Sales are $100,800 and cost of sales is $72,000
D   Sales are $100,800 and cost of sales is $60,480

7   A company has the following current assets and liabilities at 31 October 20X8:

			$'000
Current assets:	inventory		970
	receivables		380
	bank		40
			1,390
Current liabilities	payables		420

When measured against accepted 'norms', the company can be said to have:

A   a high current ratio and an ideal acid test ratio

B   an ideal current ratio and a low acid test ratio

C   a high current ratio and a low acid test ratio

D   ideal current and acid test ratios

---

8   Your company's income statement for the year ended 30 September 20X8 showed the following:

	$'000
Net profit before interest and tax	1,200
Interest	200
	1,000
Corporation tax	400
Retained profit for the year	600

Its statement of financial position at 30 September 20X7 showed the following capital:

	$'000
Share capital	8,000
Retained profits balance	1,200
	9,200
10% loan stocks	2,000
	11,200

Return on average capital employed for the year ended 30 September 20X8 is

A   5.88%

B   10.17%

C   10.43%

D   none of these

---

9   An increase in both receivables' and payables' payment periods could result in:

A   An increase in working capital

B   A decrease in working capital

C   An increase in current assets and current liabilities

D   A decrease in current assets and current liabilities

10   The gearing ratio is often calculated as

    A   Long-term loans and current liabilities as a percentage of total shareholders' funds
    B   Current and long-term debt as a percentage of total net assets
    C   Long-term loans and preference shares as a percentage of total shareholders' funds
    D   Preference shares as a percentage of equity capital

31 Ratios II

1   What is the ideal current ratio for a business?

    A   1:1
    B   2:1
    C   It is the trend which is important.
    D   It does not matter provided the business can pay its way.

2   Which of the following factors would indicate a lowering of the current ratio? (Assume all other elements of working capital are unaffected for each option.)

    A   A decrease in the rate of inventory turnover (measured as a multiple) ie 10 times pa to 6 times pa.
    B   An increasing bank overdraft
    C   A decrease in the bank overdraft
    D   An increase in the period of credit allowed to credit customers

3   A company has the following extract from its statement of financial position: debentures $2.5 million, ordinary shares $1.5 million, preference shares $0.5 million, reserves $2.2 million, share premium account $0.2 million. Using a conventional approach calculate the gearing %.

    A   147%
    B   77%
    C   39%
    D   44%

Use these summarised accounts to answer Questions 4 to 10

Summarised statement of financial position at 31 December 20X4

		$'000	$'000
Non-current assets			4,700
Current assets:	Inventory	1,200	
	Receivables	1,700	
	Cash	300	
			3,200
			7,900

	$'000
Capital and reserves	
Ordinary $1 share capital	2,000
Preference share capital	400
Retained profits	1,000
	3,400
10% loan stock	3,000
Current liabilities	
Payables	1,500
	7,900

Summarised income statement at 31 December 20X4

	£'000
Turnover	12,000
Cost of sales	7,000
Gross profit	5,000
Operating expenses	(2,500)
Operating profit	2,500
Debenture interest	(300)
Profit before taxation	2,200
Taxation	(700)
	1,500
Preference dividend	20

4   Return on capital employed is:

    A   34%

    B   39%

    C   65%

    D   73%

5   Asset turnover is:

    A   0.781 times
    B   1.875 times
    C   2.553 times
    D   3.529 times

6   The gross and net profit margins are:

	Gross	Net
A	21%	42%
B	71%	36%
C	42%	36%
D	42%	21%

7   Inventory days and receivables days are:

	Inventory days	Receivables days
A	36	52
B	36	88
C	62	52
D	62	88

8   The length of the cash cycle is:

    A   36 days
    B   68 days
    C   88 days
    D   192 days

9   The current ratio and the gearing ratio are:

	Current ratio	Gearing ratio
A	2.13	47%
B	2.13	53%
C	47%	2.13
D	68%	50%

10   The payable days are:

    A   75 days
    B   78 days
    C   36 days
    D   68 days

Objective test questions

1 Ledger accounting and books of prime entry I

1   Your organisation sold goods to PQ for $800 less trade discount of 20% and cash discount of 5% for payment within 14 days. The invoice was settled by cheque five days later. What is the double entry for the cash discount allowed?

Debit	Credit
$	$
....	....

2   The following totals appear in the day books for March 20X8.

	Goods excluding Sales tax	Sales tax
	$	$
Sales day book	40,000	7,000
Purchases day book	20,000	3,500
Returns inwards day book	2,000	350
Returns outward day book	4,000	700

Opening and closing inventories are both $3,000.

The gross profit for March 20X8 is ....

3   Diesel fuel in inventory at 1 November 20X7 was $12,500, and there were invoices awaited for $1,700. During the year to 31 October 20X8, diesel fuel bills of $85,400 were paid, and a delivery worth $1,300 had yet to be invoiced. At 31 October 20X8, the inventory of diesel fuel was valued at $9,800.

The diesel fuel to be charged to the income statement for the year to 31 October 20X8 is

....

4   An increase in the allowance for receivables results in a decrease in .... and

increases/decreases the profit for the year (circle as appropriate).

5   The petty cash imprest is restored to $100 at the end of each week. The following amounts are paid out of petty cash during week 23.

Stationery	$14.10 including sales tax at 17.5%
Travelling costs	$25.50
Office refreshments	$12.90
Sundry payables	$24.00 plus sales tax at 17.5%

The amount required to restore the imprest to $100 is ....

6   A company's telephone bill consists of two elements. One is a quarterly rental charge, payable in advance; the other is a quarterly charge for calls made, payable in arrears. At 1 April 20X9, the previous bill dated 1 March 20X9 had included line rental of $90. Estimated call charges during March 20X9 were $80.

During the following 12 months, bills totalling $2,145 were received on 1 June, 1 September, 1 December 20X9 and 1 March 20Y0, each containing rental of $90 as well as call charges. Estimated call charges for March 20Y0 were $120.

The amount to be charged to the income statement for the year ended 31 March 20Y0 is

....

The following data relates to questions 7-10

At 1 October 20X5, the following balances were brought forward in the ledger accounts of XY:

Rent payable account	Dr	$1,000
Electricity account	Cr	$800
Interest receivable account	Dr	$300
Allowance for receivables	Cr	$4,800

You are told the following.

(a)   Rent is payable quarterly in advance on the last day of November, February, May and August, at the rate of $6,000 per annum.

(b)   Electricity is paid as follows.

5 November 20X5	$1,000 (for the period to 31 October 20X5)
10 February 20X6	$1,300 (for the period to 31 January 20X6)
8 May 20X6	$1,500 (for the period to 30 April 20X6)
7 August 20X6	$1,100 (for the period to 31 July 20X6)

At 30 September 20X6, the electricity meter shows that $900 has been consumed since the last bill was received.

(c)   Interest was received during the year as follows.

2 October 20X5	$250 (for the six months to 30 September 20X5)
3 April 20X6	$600 (for the six months to 31 March 20X6)

You estimate that interest of $300 is accrued at 30 September 20X6.

(d)   At 30 September 20X6, the balance of receivables amounts to $125,000. The allowance for receivables is to be amended to 5% of receivables.

7   The rent charge to the income statement for the year is $ ....

8   The charge for electricity to the income statement for the year is $ ....

9   The amount of interest receivable to appear in the income statement for the year is

     $ ....

10   The charge or credit to the income statement for allowance for receivables is $ ....

     Charge/credit (circle as appropriate)

2 Ledger accounting and books of prime entry II

The following data relates to questions 1 to 6

Your organisation has recently employed a new accounts assistant who is unsure about the correct use of books of original entry and the need for adjustments to be made to the accounts at the end of the year. You have been asked to give the new assistant some guidance.

For each of the following examples of transactions to be recorded in the books of original entry complete the double entry posting sheet below.

1   Purchase of raw materials on credit from J Burgess, list price $27,000 less trade discount of 33 1/3 %, plus sales tax of 17.5%.

2   Payment to a payable, P Barton, by cheque in respect of a debt of $14,000, less cash discount of 2%.

3   Receipt of a piece of office equipment in payment of a debt of $2,500 from a receivable, J Smithers.

4   Write off a debt of $500 due from A Scholes.

5   Returns of goods sold to J Lockley, total invoice value of $470, including sales tax of 17.5%.

6   Purchase of a motor vehicle on credit from A Jackson, for $1,400, including road fund (vehicle licence) tax of $75.

DOUBLE ENTRY POSTING SHEET

ITEM	BOOK OF ORIGINAL ENTRY	DEBIT ENTRIES Account	$	CREDIT ENTRIES Account	$
(i)					
(ii)					
(iii)					
(iv)					
(v)					
(vi)					

The following data relates to questions 7 to 8

Business rates are paid annually on 1 April, to cover the following 12 months. The business rates for 20X1/X2 are $1,800, and for 20X2/20X3 are increased by 20%. Rent is paid quarterly on the first day of May, August, November and February, in arrears. The rent has been $1,200 per annum for some time, but increases to $1,600 per annum from 1 February 20X2.

7   The charge for business rates in the income statement for the year ended 30 April 20X2 is

     $ ....

8   The charge for rent in the income statement for the year ended 30 April 20X2 is $ ....

3 Conceptual and regulatory framework

1   It has been suggested that there are seven separate user groups of published accounting statements. These include owner/investors, loan payables, analysts/advisors, business contacts (for example customers and suppliers) and the public. Which two are missing?

     1   ....

     2   ....

2   Dee has given you a piece of paper with two statements about accounting concepts.

     (a)   A business continues in existence for the foreseeable future.
     (b)   Revenues and expenses should be recognised in the period in which they are earned or incurred.

     Required

     Name the two accounting concepts described above.

     1   ....

     2   ....

3   The following statement describes an accounting concept. 'In conditions of uncertainty more confirmatory evidence is required about the existence of an asset or a gain than about the existence of a liability or a loss.'

     Which accounting concept is being described here? ....

4   A business has incurred the following expenses. You are to complete the table indicating whether the expenditure is capital expenditure or revenue expenditure.

	Capital expenditure	Revenue expenditure
Redecoration of factory		
New engine for machinery		
Cleaning of factory		
Purchase of delivery van		

5   Closing inventories are deducted from purchases and opening inventories in the income statement in order to determine the cost of sales. Of which accounting concept is this an example?

    ....

6   Accounting standards are issued by the Financial Reporting Council.

    True or False?

4 Non-current assets

1   A machine cost $9,000. It has an expected useful life of six years, and an expected residual value of $1,000. It is to be depreciated at 30% per annum on the reducing balance basis. A full year's depreciation is charged in the year of purchase, with none in the year of sale. During year 4, it is sold for $3,000.

    The profit or loss on disposal is ....

2   The accounting concept which dictates that non-current assets should be valued at cost, less accumulated

    depreciation, rather than their enforced saleable value, is the .... concept.

3   A non-current asset was disposed of for $2,200 during the last accounting year. It had been purchased exactly three years earlier for $5,000, with an expected residual value of $500, and had been depreciated on the reducing balance basis, at 20% per annum.

    The profit or loss on disposal was ....

4   By charging depreciation in the accounts, a business aims to ensure that the cost of non-current assets is

    spread .... which benefit from their use.

5   A machine was purchased in 20X6 for $64,000. It was expected to last for 5 years and to have a residual value of $2,000. Depreciation was charged at 50% per annum on the reducing balance method, with a full year's charge in the year of purchase. No depreciation is charged in the year of disposal. The company's year end is 31 December. The machine was sold on 3 April 20Y0 for $5,500. The profit or loss on sale is

    ....

The following data relates to questions 6 and 7

On 1 January 20X1 a business purchased a laser printer costing $1,800. The printer has an estimated life of 4 years after which it will have no residual value.

6   Calculate the depreciation charge for 20X2 on the laser printer on the straight line basis:

    ....

    ....

7   Calculate the depreciation charge for 20X2 on the laser printer on the reducing balance basis at 60% per annum

....

....

5 Inventories

1   IAS 2 recognises two main ways of calculating cost of inventories. What are they? Complete the blanks below

1   ....

2   ....

The following data relates to questions 2 to 4

The trading account of T is set out below:

T
Trading Account for the year ended 30 April 20X1

	$'000	$'000
Turnover		1,000
Opening inventory	200	
Purchases	700	
	900	
Closing inventory	300	
Cost of goods sold		600
Gross profit		400

The opening and closing inventory in T Co was valued on a FIFO basis. On a LIFO basis the opening and closing inventory would have been valued at $180,000 and $270,000 respectively.

2   The gross profit if LIFO had been used for inventory valuation would have been $ ....

3   What are the 'inventory days', using average inventory during the year, on the assumption that inventory is valued on the FIFO basis?

....

....

....

....

4	What are the 'inventory days', using the average method, on the assumption that inventory is valued on the LIFO basis?

....

....

....

....

6 Bank reconciliations

The following data relates to questions 1 and 2

On 10 January 20X9, Jane Smith received her monthly bank statement for December 20X8. The statement showed the following.

SOUTHERN BANK PLC

Date	Particulars	Debits	Credits	Balance
	J Smith: Statement of Account			
20X8		$	$	$
Dec 1	Balance			1,862
Dec 5	417864	243		1,619
Dec 5	Dividend		26	1,645
Dec 5	Bank Giro Credit		212	1,857
Dec 8	417866	174		1,683
Dec 10	417867	17		1,666
Dec 11	Sundry Credit		185	1,851
Dec 14	Standing Order	32		1,819
Dec 20	417865	307		1,512
Dec 20	Bank Giro Credit		118	1,630
Dec 21	417868	95		1,535
Dec 21	417870	161		1,374
Dec 24	Bank charges	18		1,356
Dec 27	Bank Giro Credit		47	1,403
Dec 28	Direct Debit	88		1,315
Dec 29	417873	12		1,303
Dec 29	Bank Giro Credit		279	1,582
Dec 31	417871	25		1,557

Her cash book for the corresponding period showed:

CASH BOOK

20X8		$	20X8		Cheque no	$
Dec 1	Balance b/d	1,862	Dec 1	Electricity	864	243
Dec 4	J Shannon	212	Dec 2	P Simpson	865	307
Dec 9	M Lipton	185	Dec 5	D Underhill	866	174
Dec 19	G Hurst	118	Dec 6	A Young	867	17
Dec 26	M Evans	47	Dec 10	T Unwin	868	95
Dec 27	J Smith	279	Dec 14	B Oliver	869	71
Dec 29	V Owen	98	Dec 16	Rent	870	161
Dec 30	K Walters	134	Dec 20	M Peters	871	25
			Dec 21	L Philips	872	37
			Dec 22	W Hamilton	873	12
			Dec 31	Balance c/d		1,793
		2,935				2,935

1   Calculate the corrected cash book balance as at 31 December 20X8:

    ....

2   Fill in the missing words and figures.

    To reconcile the balance per the bank statement at 31 December 20X8 with the corrected cashbook balance at that date:

    •   Add .... of $ .... ; and

    •   Deduct .... of $ ....

The following data relates to question 3

Sandilands uses a computer package to maintain its accounting records. A printout of its cash book for the month of May 20X3 was extracted on 31 May and is summarised below.

	$		$
Opening balance	546	Payments	335,966
Receipts	336,293	Closing balance	873
	336,839		336,839

The company's chief accountant provides you with the following information.

(a)   The company's bank statement for May was received on 1 June and showed an overdrawn balance of $1,444 at the end of May.

(b)   Cheques paid to various payables totalling $7,470 have not yet been presented to the bank.

(c)   Cheques received by Sandilands totalling $6,816 were paid into the bank on 31 May but not credited by the bank until 2 June.

(d)   Bank charges of $630 shown on the bank statement have not been entered in the company's cash book.

(e) Standing orders entered on the bank statement totalling $2,584 have not been recorded in the company's cash book.

(f) A cheque drawn by Sandilands for $693 and presented to the bank on 26 May has been incorrectly entered in the cash book as $936.

3 The corrected cash book balance at 31 May is $ ....

4 At 31 December 20X9 the cash book of a company shows a credit balance of $901. When the bank statement for the month of December was compared with the cash book, it was discovered that cheques totalling $2,468 had been drawn but not presented to the bank, and cheques received totalling $593 had not yet been credited by the bank.

The balance on the bank statement at 31 December 20X9 was ....

7 Control accounts, sales tax and payroll

1 An employee is paid at the rate of $3.50 per hour. Earnings of more than $75 a week are taxed at 20%. Employees' National Insurance is 7%, and Employer's National Insurance is 10%. During week 24, the employee works for 36 hours.

The amounts to be charged to the income statement and paid to the employee are:

Income statement   Paid to employee

....

2 A receivables control account showed a debit balance of $37,642. The individual receivables' accounts in the sales ledger showed a total of $35,840. The difference could be due to entering discount allowed of

.... on the debit side of the control account.

3 A business paid out $12,450 in net wages to its employees. In respect of these wages, the following amounts were shown in the statement of financial position.

	$
Income tax payable	2,480
National Insurance payable – employees'	1,350
– employer's	1,500
Pension payable for employees' contributions	900

Employees' gross wages, before deductions, were ....

4 A debit balance of $1,250 on X's account in the books of Y means that:

X .... Y

5   A business has the following transactions for the month of June 20X2:

Credit sales (including sales tax at 17.5%)	164,500
Sales returns (including sales tax at 17.5%)	6,200
Cheques from receivables	155,300
Discounts allowed to customers	5,100
Bad debts written off	2,600

The receivables balance at 30 June 20X2 was $8,300.

The receivables balance at 1 June 20X2 was $ ....

---

6   The following totals have been extracted from the books of a business at 30 September 20X2.

	$
Sales day book total	367,520
Purchases day book total	227,540
Returns inwards day book total	13,445
Returns outwards day book total	9,045
Discounts allowed	5,220
Discounts received	2,070
Cash receipts from receivables	361,200
Cash payments to payables	210,040

The payables control account had a balance of $17,600 at 1 September 20X2. During the month a journal entry has recorded a contra entry between a receivables account and a payables account of $940.

The balance on the payables control account at 30 September 20X2 is $ ....

---

8 Correction of errors and suspense accounts

1   An organisation restores its petty cash balance to $250 at the end of each month. During October, the total expenditure column in the petty cash book was calculated as being $210, and the imprest was restored by this amount. The analysis columns posted to the nominal ledger totalled only $200.

This error would result in the trial balance being $10 higher on the .... side.

---

2   A trial balance has an excess of debits over credits of $14,000 and a suspense account has been opened to make it balance. It is later discovered that:

(a)   The discounts allowed balance of $3,000 and the discounts received balance of $7,000 have both been entered on the wrong side of the trial balance.

(b)   The payables control account balance of $233,786 had been included in the trial balance as $237,386.

(c)   An item of $500 had been omitted from the sales records (ie from the sales day book).

(d)   The balance on the current account with the senior partner's wife had been omitted from the trial balance. This item when corrected removes the suspense account altogether.

The balance on the current account with the senior partner's wife is $ ....

The following data relates to questions 3 to 11

After calculating net profit for the year ended 31 March 20X8, WL has the following trial balance.

	DR $	CR $
Land and buildings – cost	10,000	
Land and buildings – depreciation at 31 March 20X8		2,000
Plant – cost	12,000	
Plant – depreciation at 31 March 20X8		3,000
Inventories	2,500	
Receivables	1,500	
Bank	8,250	
Payables		1,700
Rent prepaid	400	
Wages accrued		300
Capital account		19,400
Profit for the year ended 31 March 20X8		9,750
	34,650	36,150

A suspense account was opened for the difference in the trial balance.

Immediately after production of the above, the following errors were discovered:

(i)   A payable's account had been debited with a $300 sales invoice (which had been correctly recorded in the sales account).

(ii) The heat and light account had been credited with gas paid $150.

(iii) G Gordon had been credited with a cheque received from G Goldman for $800. Both are receivables.

(iv) The insurance account contained a credit entry for insurance prepaid of $500, but the balance had not been carried down and hence had been omitted from the above trial balance.

(v)   Purchase returns had been over-cast by $700 when posting to the purchases returns account.

---

3   Prepare a journal entry to correct error (i).

	DR $	CR $
....	....	
....		....

---

4   Prepare a journal entry to correct error (ii).

	DR $	CR $
....	....	
....		....

---

5   Prepare a journal entry to correct error (iii).

                                                                   DR   CR
                                                                   $ $

     ....

     ....

6   Prepare a journal entry to correct error (iv).

                                                                   DR   CR
                                                                   $ $

     ....

     ....

7   Prepare a journal entry to correct error (v).

                                                                   DR   CR
                                                                   $ $

     ....

     ....

8   The net profit for the year after correction of errors (i) to (v) is $ ....

9   The figure for receivables in the amended statement of financial position is $ ....

10   The figure for prepayments in the amended statement of financial position is $ ....

11   The figure for payables in the amended statement of financial position is $ ....

9 Final accounts and audit I

The following data relates to questions 1 to 3

The following trial balance has been extracted from the ledger of Mr Yousef, a sole trader.

TRIAL BALANCE AS AT 31 MAY 20X6

	Dr $	Cr $
Sales		138,078
Purchases	82,350	
Carriage	5,144	
Drawings	7,800	
Rent and insurance	6,622	
Postage and stationery	3,001	
Advertising	1,330	
Salaries and wages	26,420	
Bad debts	877	
Allowance for receivables		130
Receivables	12,120	
Payables		6,471
Cash in hand	177	
Cash at bank	1,002	
Inventory as at 1 June 20X5	11,927	
Equipment		
At cost	58,000	
Accumulated depreciation		19,000
Capital		53,091
	216,770	216,770

The following additional information as at 31 May 20X6 is available.

(a) Rent is accrued by $210.
(b) Insurance has been prepaid by $880.
(c) $2,211 of carriage represents carriage inwards on purchases.
(d) Equipment is to be depreciated at 15% per annum using the straight line method.
(e) The allowance for receivables is to be increased by $40.
(f) Inventory at the close of business has been valued at $13,551.

---

1   The gross profit for the year is $ ....

---

2   The rent and insurance charge for the year is $ ....

---

3   Fill in the figures.

Summarised statement of financial position at 31 May 20X6

	$	$
Non-current assets		....
Current assets	....	
Less: Current liabilities	....	
Net current assets		....
Total assets less current liabilities		....

4   At 1 November 20X8, a club's membership subscriptions account show a debit balance of $200 and a credit balance of $90. During the year ended 31 October 20X9, subscriptions received amounted to $4,800. At 31 October 20X9, subscriptions paid in advance amounted to $85 and subscriptions in arrears (expected to be collected) to $50.

The amount to be transferred to the income and expenditure account in respect of subscriptions for the year ended 31 October 20X9 is ....

5   The *accumulated fund* represents ....

....

The following data relates to questions 6 to 11

Miss Anne Teek runs a market stall selling old pictures, china, copper goods and curios of all descriptions. Most of her sales are for cash although regular customers are allowed credit. No double entry accounting records have been kept, but the following information is available.

SUMMARY OF NET ASSETS AT 31 MARCH 20X8

	$	$
Motor van		
Cost	3,000	
Depreciation	2,500	
Net book value		500
Current assets		
Inventory	500	
Receivables	170	
Cash at bank	2,800	
Cash in hand	55	
	3,525	
Less current liabilities		
Payables	230	
Net current assets		3,295
		3,795

Additional information

(a) Anne bought a new motor van in January 20X9 receiving a part exchange allowance of $1,800 for her old van. A full year's depreciation is to be provided on the new van, calculated at 20% on cost.

(b) Anne has taken $50 cash per week for her personal use. She also estimates that petrol for the van, paid in cash, averages $10 per week.

(c) Other items paid in cash were as follows.

Sundry expenses	$24
Repairs to stall canopy	$201

(d) Anne makes a gross profit of 40% on selling prices. She is certain that no goods have been stolen but remembers that she appropriated a set of glasses and some china for her own use. These items had a total selling price of $300.

(e) Trade receivables and payables at 31 March 20X9 are $320 and $233 respectively, and cash in hand amounts to $39. No inventory count has been made and there are no accrued or prepaid expenses.

A summary of bank statements for the twelve months in question shows the following.

Credits	$
Cash banked (all cash sales)	7,521
Cheques banked (all credit sales)	1,500
Dividend income	210
	9,231

Debits	$
Purchase of motor van	3,200
Road fund licence	80
Insurance on van	323
Payables for purchases	7,777
Rent	970
Sundry	31
Accountancy fees (re current work)	75
Bank overdraft interest (six months to 1 October 20X8)	20
Returned cheque (bad debt)	29
	12,505

The bank statement for 1 April 20X9 shows an interest charge of $27.

Assume a 52 week year.

6   The cash sales for the year were $ ....

7   The credit sales for the year were $ ....

8   The purchases for the year to be included in the trading account were $ ....

9   The van depreciation charge for the year was $ ....

10   The profit or loss on disposal of the old van was $ ....

11   The van depreciation charge and the profit or loss on disposal of the old van must be taken into account in arriving at the net profit or loss for the year. What is the **total** of the **other expenses** that are deducted from gross profit to give the net profit for the year ended 31 March 20X9? ....

10 Final accounts and audit II

1   Opening inventory is $1,000, purchases are $10,000 and sales are $15,000. The gross profit margin is 30%. Closing inventory is $ ....

2   The following information is for the year ended 31 October 20X0.

	$
Purchases of raw materials	56,000
Returns inwards	4,000
Increase in inventory of raw materials	1,700
Direct wages	21,000
Carriage inwards	2,500
Production overheads	14,000
Decrease in work-in-progress	5,000

The value of factory cost of goods completed is ....

The following data relates to questions 3 and 4

Balances at 31 December 20X4

	$
Non-current assets (cost $60,000)	39,000
Inventories	
Raw materials	25,000
Work in progress, valued at prime cost	5,800
Finished goods	51,000

The following relevant transactions occurred during 20X5.

	$
Invoiced purchases of raw materials, less returns	80,000
Discounts received	1,700
Factory wages paid	34,000
Manufacturing expenses paid	61,900

Balances at 31 December 20X5

	$
Non-current assets (cost $90,000)	60,000
Inventories	
Raw materials	24,000
Work in progress	5,000
Finished goods	52,000

3   The prime cost of production for the year was $ ....

4   The total depreciation charge for the year was $ ....

5   At the beginning of the year in GHI, the opening work in progress was $240,000. During the year the following expenditure was incurred:

	$
Prime cost	720,000
Factory overheads	72,000

The closing work in progress was $350,000.

The factory cost of goods completed during the year was $ ....

6   At the start of the year a manufacturing company had inventories of raw materials of $18,000 and inventories of finished goods of $34,000. There was no work in progress.

During the year the following expenses were incurred:

	$
Raw materials purchased	163,000
Manufacturing expenses incurred	115,000

During the year sales of $365,000 were made. The inventories of raw materials at the year end were valued at $21,000 and the inventories of finished goods were valued at $38,000. There was no work in progress.

The gross profit for the year is $ ....

7   A company made a profit for the year of $18,750, after accounting for depreciation of $1,250. During the year, non-current assets were purchased for $8,000, receivables increased by $1,000, inventory decreased by $1,800 and payables increased by $350.

The increase in cash and bank balances during the year was ....

11 Interpretation of accounts I

The following data relates to questions 1 and 2

KK has made a profit before tax of $445,000. There is to be a provision for tax for the year of $111,000 and a transfer to general reserve of $30,000. During the year an interim dividend of $40,000 was paid. Trade payables and accruals totalled $17,000.

1   The retained profit for the year was $ ....

2   The total payables to be shown in the statement of financial position were $ ....

The following data relates to questions 3 to 6

Given below are extracts from the trial balance of FG at 31 March 20X2 after preparation of the draft income statement.

	$
Share capital (50 cents ordinary shares)	200,000
Share premium account	40,000
General reserve	20,000
Retained profits reserve at 31 March 20X2	84,000

Since preparation of the draft income statement it has been discovered that three items had not been accounted for.

(i)   On 1 April 20X1 the company issued 100,000 new ordinary shares at a price of 80 cents per share.
(ii)   Closing inventory had been over stated by $10,000.
(iii)   The directors wished to make a transfer to the general reserve of $5,000.

---

3   The amended balance on the retained profits reserve at 31 March 20X2 was $ ....

Fill in the figures below.

	$
4 Share capital	....
5 Share premium	....
6 General reserve	....

---

7   A company had the following gross profit calculation in its last accounting period.

	$
Sales	130,000
Cost of sales	60,000
Gross profit	70,000

Average inventory during that period was $7,500.

In the next accounting period sales are expected to increase by 40%, and the rate of inventory turnover is expected to double. If average inventory remains at $7,500 the gross profit mark-up percentage will be .... %.

---

8   The gross profit mark-up is .... % where sales are $240,000 and cost of sales is $150,000.

The following data relates to questions 9 and 10

The following figures have been extracted from the published accounts of MBC, at 31 October 20X5.

	$m
Ordinary share capital	30
Share premium	3
Reserves	5
	38
6% loan stock	10
	48

The net profit (after tax of $1m) for the year to 31 October 20X5 was $4m and dividends amounted to $0.5m.

9   Calculate the company's gearing ratio.

....

....

10   Calculate the company's return on average capital employed (ROCE).

....

....

12 Interpretation of accounts II

The following data relates to questions 1 to 7

ARH has the following results for the last two years of trading.

ARH
INCOME STATEMENT FOR THE YEAR ENDED

	31.12.X4	31.12.X5
	$'000	$'000
Sales	14,400	17,000
Less cost of sales	11,800	12,600
Gross profit	2,600	4,400
Less expenses	1,000	2,000
Less interest	200	–
Net profit for the year	1,400	2,400
Dividends paid	520	780

ARH
STATEMENT OF FINANCIAL POSITION

	31 December 20X4		31 December 20X5	
	$'000	$'000	$'000	$'000
Non-current assets		2,500		4,000
Current assets				
Inventories	1,300		2,000	
Receivables	2,000		1,600	
Bank balances	2,400		820	
		5,700		4,420
		8,200		8,420
Financed by:				
2.4 million ordinary shares of $1 each		2,400		2,400
Revaluation reserves		500		500
Retained profits		1,200		2,820
		4,100		5,720
Long term liabilities				
10% loan stock		2,600		–
Current liabilities				
Payables		1,500		2,700
		8,200		8,420

1   The gross profit margin is

20X4	20X5
%	%
....	....

2   The net profit margin is

20X4	20X5
%	%
....	....

3   The return on capital employed is

20X4	20X5
....	....

4   The acid test ratio is

20X4	20X5
....	....

5   The asset turnover is

	20X4	20X5
	....	....

6   The inventory turnover period in days is

	20X4	20X5
	Days	Days
	....	....

7   The gearing ratio is

	20X4	20X5
	%	%
	....	....

Answers to
Multiple choice questions

1 Introduction to financial accounting

1	B	Remember you were asked for the *main* aim.
2	C	Overstating profits and understating statement of financial position asset values.
3	D	Improvements are capital expenditure, repairs and maintenance are not.
4	A	Shareholders and government are users of accounts.
5	D	Correct. This is not an objective from the statement of principles. Additional data is required to assess this.
	A	This is a primary objective.
	B	Again, a major objective.
	C	All classes of users require information for decision making.
6	A	Correct. This information is a need for the 'lender' group.
	B	This is an important need, particularly relative to other investment opportunities.
	C	A primary need.
	D	A major need for existing (and prospective) investors.

2 Basic bookkeeping I

1	A	A credit balance in the books of X means that X owes Y this amount ie Y is a payable of X.
2	C	Trade discounts are not included in the cost of purchases.
3	C	Sales less returns inwards. Discounts allowed are shown as a deduction from gross profit.
4	B	Correct, invoices are listed on receipt.
	A	Incorrect, these are recorded in a memorandum column in the cash book prior to posting to Payables accounts and the discount received account.
	C	Incorrect, the supplier will deduct trade discounts prior to raising the invoice total.
	D	They would be recorded in the purchase returns day book in response to debit notes raised on suppliers.
5	D	Remember the receivables account is a memorandum account.
6	A	The total of the cash paid column should be credited to the cash control account, and the total of the discounts received column to the credit of discounts received, and debited to the payables control account.
7	D	When cash is received by a business, a debit entry is made in the cashbook. A receipt of cash decreases an overdraft and increases a bank balance.

8 C Correct, the sales tax a/c is a personal a/c with the tax authorities.

   A Incorrect, the sales tax a/c has not been used to record the output tax charged.

   B Incorrect, the $200 represents the amount chargeable to sales tax.

   D Incorrect, a complete reversal has occurred and the nominal account involved is incorrect (payables record purchase ledger transactions).

9 D A liability or a revenue.

10 C The sales ledger. This is posted from the sales day book and cash book.

3 Basic bookkeeping II

1 C Ledger accounts are posted from books of prime entry.

2 C A = L + C. Remember that profit = I – E.

3 B

	$
Opening capital	10,000
Capital introduced	4,000
Drawings	(8,000)
Loss (bal fig)	(1,500)
Closing capital	4,500

4 D You are told that X is a receivable of Y. Therefore X normally owes Y money. Options B and C would imply that Y is a receivable of X and so can be ignored. Option A would increase the debit entry. Only option D would generate a credit entry.

4 Concepts

1 A Fails to take account of changing price levels over time.

2 D Current purchasing power accounting.

3 C Assets less liabilities = opening capital plus profits less drawings.

      ∴ Assets less liabilities less opening capital plus drawings = profit

4 D Separate entity concept. A business is separate from its owner.

5 A Accruals concept.

6 D Once capital has been maintained, anything earned in excess is profit.

7 B This is just a rewording of a previous question, be careful with these in the exam.

8 C Depreciation is an *application* of the accruals concept.

9 C In this way receivables are not overstated and accounts can be compared between periods.

10 C Only realised profits can be included in the Income statement.

11   A   Depreciation allocates the cost of an asset to the periods expected to benefit from its use.

12   B   Accruals. The stationery must be charged to the period in which it was   consumed.

5 Accruals and prepayments

1   C   Prepayment b/f $900 (9/12 × $1,200) + $1,600 – prepayment c/f $1,200 (9/12 × $1,600).

2   C

	$
Opening Inventory	165
Purchases (1,350 – 80 + 70)	1,340
	1,505
Closing Inventory	140
Stationery in income statement	1,365

3   C   On a cash basis

	$
Sales	400
Purchases	200
Profit	200

On an accruals basis

	$
Sales	1,000
Purchases	500
Profit	500

Thus, the difference is $300.

4   C

Electricity expense account

		1,000	b/d
		4,200	Income statement charge
Cash	4,000		
C/d	1,200		
	5,200	5,200	
		1,200	B/d

5   A $8,400 for 24 months is $350 per month. So, the charge for the year is 12 × $350, ie $4,200.

At 31/12/X2, rent has been prepaid to 31.12.X3 ie for 9 months which is 9 × $350 ie $3,150.

6   B

Rent received income account

B/d	1,000	5,000	Cash
Income statement	4,500	500	C/d
	5,500	5,500	

7	A		Motor expenses account			
		Cash	4,000	1,500	B/d	
				5,000	Income statement	
		C/d	2,500			
			6,500	6,500		
				2,500	B/d	

8	A		MOTOR EXPENSES				
				$			$
		1.9	Prepayment b/d	80	1.9	Accrual b/d	95
			Cash	95	30.9	Prepayment (80 ×3/4)c/d	60
			Cash	245		Income statement	385
		30.9	Accrual c/d	120			
				540			540

9	A		Rent received income account			
		B/d	1,000	16,000	Cash	
		Income statement	12,000			
		C/d	3,000			
			16,000	16,000		
				3,000	B/d	

10 D Prepayments are included in current assets. A is wrong as bad debts are an example of the prudence concept. Prepayments reduce expenses and so increase profits, so C is wrong. This leaves a choice between B and D, with D being the correct option.

6 Non-current assets I

1 A It is **never** B as funds are not set aside; nor C, this is revaluation.

2 D ($5,000 − $1,000)/4 = $1,000 depreciation per annum ∴NBV = $2,000.

3 D

	$
Balance b/d	67,460
Less NBV of non-current asset sold	
15,000 − (15,000 − (4,000 + 1,250))	5,250
	62,210

4 A If disposal proceeds were $15,000 and profit on disposal is $5,000, then net book value must be $10,000, the difference between the non-current asset register figure and the non-current asset account in the nominal ledger.

5 A The stationery would appear as an asset rather than as an expense

6 C Compare this with the answers to 1 above

7	C			$
		Profit		8,000
		Add back: depreciation		12,000
		Net cash inflow		20,000
		Purchase of non-current assets for cash		(25,000)
		Decrease in cash		5,000

8   A   We would need to know *either* sale proceeds *or* length of time in order to calculate the other.

9   A   *Ledger accounts*

	$
As at 1.1.X7	
Cost	60,000
Depreciation	15,000
	45,000

Non-current asset register

At 1.1.X7	
Net book value	47,500
Disposal of asset which cost $(4,000 + 1,500)	(5,500)
	42,000

10	B			$
		Year 1	Purchase	2,400.00
		Year 1	Depreciation	(480.00)
				1,920.00
		Year 2	Depreciation	(384.00)
				1,536.00
		Year 3	Depreciation	(307.20)
				1,228.80
		Year 4	Sale proceeds	1,200.00
			Loss on disposal	(28.80)

7 Non-current assets II

1	A		$	$
		Net book value at 1st August 20X8		200,000
		Less depreciation		(20,000)
		Proceeds	25,000	
		Loss	5,000	
		Therefore net book value		(30,000)
				150,000

2   C   Correct, it is likely to be treated as capital expenditure.

    A   This is a repair, so it is revenue expenditure.

    B   This is a repair and renewal expense so it would be likely to be treated as a revenue item.

    D   Incorrect, these are unlikely to be sufficiently expensive to warrant treatment as capital expenditure.

3	C			$
		31/7/20X5	Cost	20,000
		Year to 31/12/X5	Depreciation	4,000
		Year to 31/12/X6	Depreciation	4,000
		Year to 31/12/X7	Depreciation	4,000
		Year to 31/12/X8	Depreciation	4,000
		Net book value at date of sale		4,000
		Sale proceeds		5,500
		Profit on disposal		1,500

4   A   The assets has been depreciated for 4 years (X5, X6, X7 and X8).

	$
Sales proceeds	5,500
Profit on disposal	1,500
Net book value at disposal	4,000
Cost	20,000
Depreciation to date	16,000

ie $4,000 pa which is 20% of $20,000.

5   B

	$
Cost	15,000
1st year depreciation	(2,250)
Net book value	12,750
2nd year depreciation	1,913
Net book value	10,837

6   A   The credit must go to a revaluation reserve.

7   D   Shares would be included in investments.

8 Bad debts and allowances for receivables

1   D   A decrease in the allowance is written back to profit.

2   A   The debt needs to be written off. The allowance previously made will be adjusted at the year end.

3   C   Correct, an increase in the allowance for receivables will reduce profits and receivables.

     D   Incorrect, gross profit will not be affected since allowances for receivables are dealt with in the net profit section.

4   D

Allowance

		3,000	b/d
Bad debt expense	2,000		
Allowance c/d	1,000		
	3,000	3,000	

Bad debts

Write off	1,000	800	Cash
Income statement	1,800	2,000	Allowance written back
	2,800	2,800	

Total bad debt expense = $1,800 credit in the income statement account.

5   B

Allowance account

		1,000	b/d
C/d	1,640	640	Movement
	1,640	1,640	

Allowances made

Specific B	500
F	800
General 2% × (18,500 – 1,500)	340
	1,640

6   D   Prudence. The provision prevents receivables being overstated.

7   C

Allowance

		850	b/d
C/d	1,000		
		150	Expense
	1,000	1,000	

Bad debts expense

Allowance	150		
Receivables	500	650	Income statement
	650	650	

9 Cost of goods sold and inventories I

1   D   Gross profit – expenses = net profit.

2   C

	$
Purchases	10,000
Less purchase returns	(200)
	9,800
Add carriage inwards	1,500
Add opening Inventory	1,000
Less closing Inventory	(2,000)
Cost of sales	10,300

Note. $800 prompt payment discount received will appear as income in the Income statement. It is not deducted from cost of sales.

3   B   FIFO will treat Inventory on hand as the most recent purchases, which are the most expensive.

4   C   Cost of sales is $1,300 understated and expenses $1,000 understated.

5   C   Closing inventory = 20 units @ $3 each = $60

6   D   2 @ $3.00 + 10 @ $3.50 = $41.00

7   C

	Units	Unit cost $	Total $	Average $
Opening inventory	30	2.00	60	
5 August purchase	50	2.40	120	
	80		180	2.25
10 August issue	(40)	2.25	(90)	
	40		90	
18 August purchase	60	2.50	150	
	100		240	2.40
23 August issue	(25)	2.40	(60)	
	75		180	

8   B

		$	$
Sales			148,000
COS	Opening inventory	34,000	
	Purchases	100,000	
		134,000	
	Closing inventory (bal fig)	(26,000)	
			108,000
			40,000

		Quantity	Value
			$
9	C		
1 October (60 × $12)		60	720
8 October (40 × $15)		100	1,320
14 October (50 × $18)		150	2,220 (ie average cost $14.80)
21 October (75 × $14.80)		75	1,110

		$	No	$	Average
10	B				
Inventory card	6 @ $15	90	6	90	
	10 @ $19.80	198	16	288	18.00
	10 @ $18	(180)	6	108	18.00
	20 @ $24.50	490	26	598	23.00
	5 @ $23	(115)	21	483	

	$
Sales (15 @ $30)	450
Issues (10 @ $18 + 5 @ $23)	(295)
Profit	155

10 Cost of goods sold and inventories II

1	A	FIFO values inventory at the latest prices.
2	C	IAS 2 specifically discourages the use of LIFO and replacement costs.
3	B	Correct, $58,000 + $256,000 − $17,000 − $63,000 = $234,000.
	A	Incorrect, returns and inventory changes must be allowed for.
	C	Incorrect, changes in inventory levels must be allowed for.
	D	Incorrect, you have transposed opening and closing inventories.
4	B	Correct. This loss is not part of cost of sales.
	A	This is a reversal error.
	C	Incorrect; loss of inventory is an expense, if the inventory had been for proprietors own use then the drawings account would be used.
	D	Incorrect; the inventory has disappeared, the debit to Inventory will increase inventory!
5	B	Correct. The amount which can be realised, less any further expenses.
	A	Incorrect.
	C	Incorrect.
	D	Incorrect.

6 A Correct, FIFO will produce the highest valuation of closing inventory of the three methods, giving the higher profit figure.

B Incorrect, under LIFO costing closing inventory will be valued at the earlier prices.

C Incorrect, LIFO is not permissible under IAS 2.

D Incorrect, average cost will be recalculated after every new delivery into Inventory occurs.

7 C Correct, the inventory would be included at the lower of cost or NRV – assuming it was saleable at a profit the appropriate cost would be that relating to its finished goods state.

8 A Carriage out will come under distribution costs in the income statement.

9 B

	Quantity	Cost	Net realisable value (95% of sales price)	Valuation Per unit	total
Beads	2,000	$1.50	$1.4535	$1.4535	2,907
Buttons	1,500	$1.25	$1.33	$1.25	1,875
Bows	2,000	$1.60	$1.425	$1.425	2,850
					7,632

11 Bank reconciliations I

1 B $(565)o/d – $92 dishonoured cheque = $(657) o/d. Remember that you are asked to calculate the figure to be shown in the financial statements ie the adjusted cash book figure.

2 D The question refers to the figure to be shown in the statement of financial position.

	$	$
Balance per cash book		5,675
Reversal – Standing order entered twice	125	
Adjustment – Dishonoured cheque (450 × 2) entered in error as a debit		900
Bank overdraft	6,450	
	6,575	6,575

3 A

	$	$
Opening bank balance	2,500	
Payment ($1,000 – $200) × 90%		720
Receipt ($200 – $10)	190	
Closing bank balance		1,970
	2,690	2,690

4 B

	$	$
Balance per bank statement		800
Unpresented cheque		80
Dishonoured cheque *		–
Corrected balance	880	
	880	880

* This has already been deducted from the balance on the bank statement.

5	B		$
		Cash book balance	2,490
		Adjustment re charges	(50)
		Adjustment re dishonoured cheque	(140)
			2,300

6	B		$	$
		Bank statement balance b/d	13,400	
		Dishonoured cheque	300	
		Bank charges not in cash book	50	
		Unpresented cheques		2,400
		Uncleared bankings	1,000	
		Adjustment re error (2 × 195)		390
		Cash book balance c/d		11,960
			14,750	14,750
		Cash book balance b/d	11,960	

Alternative approach:

			$	$
		Cash book balance b/d	11,960	
		Dishonoured cheque		300
		Bank charges not in cash book		50
		Unpresented cheques	2,400	
		Uncleared bankings		1,000
		Adjustment re error (2 × 195)	390	
		Bank statement balance c/d		13,400
			14,750	14,750
		Bank statement balance b/d	13,400	

7	A		$	$
		Cash book (the cash book has a credit balance)		1,240
		Unpresented cheques	450	
		Uncleared deposit		140
		Bank charges		75
		Bank overdraft	1,005	
			1,455	1,455

8   D   Provided that the cash receipts have been correctly posted to the cash book, then the fact that they have incorrectly been posted to payables instead of cash sales or receivables will not affect the bank reconciliation.

9   D   All the other options would have the bank account $250 less than the cash book.

		$	$
10	B		
	Cash book		500
	Unpresented cheques	6,000	
	Uncleared deposit		5,000
	Bank balance		500
		6,000	6,000

12 Bank reconciliations II

1   C   When funds are paid out of a bank account, a debit entry appears on a bank statements. A payment increases an overdraft and decreases a bank balance.

2   D

	$
Balance per cash account	10,500 o/d
Less bank charges	175
Less transposition error	18
	10,693 o/d

3   B

	$
Balance per cash account	10,500 o/d
Add bank charges	175
Add transposition error	18
Adjusted cash account	10,693
Less uncleared cheques	(1,050)
	9,643 o/d

4   B   The only adjustment that should be made to the cash account is to record the bank charges. The cheques and lodgements will already have been recorded in the cash account.

5   B   The $20 advance returned can be offset against the cash requirement.

6   D   Correct.

	Cash $	Bank $	
Balance	500	(1,000)	
Receipts	12,600		
Contra	(5,500)	5,500	
Paid	(3,200)	(8,200)	
Drawings	(3,800)	(2,500)	(balancing figure) = total of $6,300
Balance	600	(6,200)	

A   Incorrect, you have recorded the contra entry incorrectly as cash withdrawn from the bank account.
B   Incorrect, you have treated the opening bank overdraft as an asset.
C   Incorrect, you have not included the contra entry in the bank workings.

7   B

CASH BOOK

	$		$
Bal b/f	5,000	Payables (98%×12,000)	11,760
Receivables	26,000	Bank charges	125
Cash sales	2,500	Bal c/f	21,615
	33,500		33,500

13 Control accounts, sales tax and payroll I

1   **D**

PAYABLES CONTROL ACCOUNT

	$		$
Bank	542,300	Balance b/d	142,600
Discounts	13,200	∴ Purchases	578,200
Returns	27,500		
Balance c/d	137,800		
	720,800		720,800

2   **C**

Receivables control account

B/d	2,500	10,600	Cash
		5,000	Contras
Sales	15,100	2,000	C/d
	17,600	17,600	

3   **D**   The charge for the salary in the Income statement is the gross salary plus the employer's national insurance contribution. This is $1,000 plus $100 respectively, a total of $1,100.

4   **D**   Businesses not registered for sales tax still have to pay sales tax.

5   **D**

	$
Opening Inventory	12,000
Purchases (bal. fig)	122,000
Purchase returns	(5,000)
Closing Inventory	(18,000)
Cost of goods sold	111,000

6   **D**

	$
Assets	
Opening cash	1,000
Cash received $(1,000 + 175 sales tax)	1,175
Closing cash	2,175
Inventory $(800 – 400)	400
	2,575
Liabilities	
Opening liabilities	–
sales tax Payable	175
Purchase inventory	800
Closing liabilities	975
Capital	
Opening capital	1,000
Profit on sale of inventory $(1,000 – 400)	600
Closing capital	1,600

7	C	Correct. 10 × $120 less 20% = invoice price $960 less cash discount 2½% ($24).
	A	This is list price less cash discount.
	B	No discounts have been applied.
	D	Cash discount not taken.

| 8 | C | Correct, the effect is double the amount concerned. |

| 9 | D | Both receivables and payables are being reduced. |

| 10 | A | Correct, receivables and payables include sales tax where applicable. |

14 Control accounts, sales tax and payroll II

1	B	Correct, all deductions will also be debited to wages control (and credited to deduction control a/c's) the balance on wages control then represents the gross wage expense.
	A	The debit to income statement represents the gross pay costs including employers overheads.
	C	Net wages will be credited to bank.
	D	Incorrect.

| 2 | C | Credit sales = $80,000 – $10,000 + $9,000 = $79,000. |

| 3 | B | All of the other options would lead to a *higher* balance in the supplier's records |

| 4 | C | Debits total $32,750 + $125,000 + $1,300 = $159,050. Credits total $1,275 + $122,550 + $550 = $124,325. ∴ Net balance = $34,725 debit. |

| 5 | A | The other options would make the credit side total $50 more than the debit side. |

| 6 | A | $8,500 – (2 × $400) = $7,700. |

| 7 | B | The trader cannot recover the sales tax so it is included in purchases |

		$
List price		2,000
Trade discount: 20%		400
		1,600
Sales tax at 17½%		280
		1,880

8	A		$
		Opening balance	34,500
		Credit purchases	78,400
		Discounts	(1,200)
		Payments	(68,900)
		Purchase returns	(4,700)
			38,100

| 9 | B | The sales tax element of the invoices will go to the sales tax account in the statement of financial position. |

| 10 | B | The cost to the business consists of gross wage plus employer's NI. |

15 Control accounts, sales tax and payroll III

			$
1	B		

$$\text{Output sales tax } \$27,612.50 \times \frac{17.5}{117.5} \qquad\qquad 4{,}112.50$$

$$\text{Input sales tax } \$18,000 \times \frac{17.5}{100} \qquad\qquad \underline{3{,}150.00}$$

∴ Balance on sales tax a/c (credit)   962.50

2   C   The same error can still appear in the control account and the personal ledger.

3   A   Correct, if the day book was overcast, the total of the purchase invoices posted to the control account will be overstated.

B   Incorrect, this would increase the difference by reducing the total of purchase ledger balances.

C   Incorrect, again this would reduce the purchase ledger total.

D   Incorrect, this would reduce the purchase ledger balance.

4   D   A credit balance treated as a debit must be subtracted twice (ie $300). An omitted debit balance must be added once. Thus, the required adjustment to the list of balances is subtract $180; no adjustment is required to the sales ledger control account.

5   A   Remember, daybook totals are posted to the control account. Individual invoices are posted to the individual accounts, so an error in a total does not affect the list of balances.

6   B   Goods returned reduce what customers owe.

7   C   Remember, daybook totals are posted to the control account. Individual invoices are posted to the individual accounts, so an error in a total does not affect the list of balances.

8   B

Receivables control account

B/d	2,050	4,000	Sales return
Sales	90,000	72,300	Cash
		2,570	Discounts allowed
		13,180	C/d
	92,050	92,050	

9   A

Receivables control account

B/d	2,050	10,000	Sales return
Sales	100,000	85,500	Cash
		1,550	Contra
		5,000	C/d
	102,050	102,050	

16 Errors and suspense accounts I

1 D $10,200 + $3,000 + $1,400 = $14,600.

2 C

	$'000
Turnover ($1m + $10,000 – $20,000)	990
Cost of sales ($800,000 – $20,000)	780
Gross profit	210

Gross profit margin = $\frac{210}{990} \times 100 = 21.2\%$

3 A Both errors will affect cost of sales and therefore gross profit, making a net effect of $40,000. Net profit will be further reduced by $10,000 missing from stationery Inventories.

4 D A and B will only affect the personal ledgers, C will cause an incorrect double   entry.

5 D Remember these are **draft** accounts. No suspense account should remain in the final accounts.

6 C An error of principle.

7 D Debits will exceed credits by 2 × $48 = $96

8 B A would give a debit balance of $130, C would have no effect and D would not cause a trial balance imbalance.

9 C Think of the double entry. Bank has been credited by $420 but expenses only debited by $400.

10 D An error of principle.

17 Errors and suspense accounts II

1 D Both these errors affect both the debit and the credit in the nominal ledger and so do not stop the trial balance balancing.

2 B Correct, carriage inwards should be treated as part of the cost of purchases in the trading account.

   A There will be no effect on net profit.

3 B Correct, the correcting journal would be

Dr	Suspense	$2,500	
Cr	Bank		$2,500

   A Incorrect, this is a reversal error which would be corrected as:

Dr	Rates	$5,000	
Cr	Bank		$5,000

   C Incorrect, an error of omission cannot create a TB difference.

   D Incorrect, this is a reversal error.

4 A

Suspense account				
B/d	450			
Discounts received	2,050	Discounts allowed	2,500	
	2,500		2,500	

5 D Discounts received should be a credit balance, but have recorded it as a debit. Thus, the suspense account is a credit of $4,100. So the required journal is:

Dr   suspense $4,100
Cr   discounts received $4,100

6 B When a debt previously written off is recovered, the correct entry is dr cash, cr bad debts expense. Thus the required journal entry is:

Dr   Receivables control $400
Cr   suspense $400

7 B A and C are errors of commission, D is an error of original entry.

8 A

SUSPENSE ACCOUNT			
	$		$
Balance b/d	210	Gas bill (420 – 240)	180
Interest	70	Discount (2 × 500)	100
	280		280

9 C A is an error of omission, B is an error of principle, D is a transposition error.

10 B The posting is correct, but the wrong amount has been used.

18 Errors and suspense accounts III

1 C This is a posting made to the wrong class of account.

2 A Closing inventory is entered twice in an extended trial balance (once for the income statement and once for the statement of financial position). It is not included in a trial balance, which, of course, balanced without it!

3 B Opening inventory is a debit balance.

4 B The journal for this transaction is debit drawings and credit purchases. Thus, profit rises and net assets stay the same.

5 A The journal for this correction is debit non-current assets, credit purchases. Thus, profit and net assets are increased.

6 D Reclassifying a liability as long term rather than current, will increase net current assets, but has no effect on current assets or net assets.

7 D This Inventory should be included at the lower of cost and net realisable value, causing profits to rise by $5,000.

19 Sole trader's accounts

1   A   Decrease = $400 + $1,200 – $250.

2   D   Correct. A margin of 20% on sales equates to a gross profit of 25% (mark up) on cost of sales. So total margin = 20% × 150,000 = 30,000. Cost of sales is 150,000 – 30,000 = 120,000. Purchases are 120,000 + 15,000 – 10,000 = $125,000.

       A   Incorrect, you have reversed the opening and closing Inventory figures.

       B   Incorrect, you have ignored the mark up entirely.

       C   Incorrect, you have applied the mark up % to sales.

3   D   In the other three cases only statement of financial position accounts are affected and there is an equal and opposite debit and credit.

4   B $9,000 is payable (income statement), but only $6,000 paid (April and July).

5   A

	$'000
Profit for the year	1,175
Add back depreciation	100
	1,275
Add issue of shares	1,000
Less repayment of debentures	(750)
Less purchase of non-current assets	(200)
	1,325
Less increase in working capital	(575)
Increase in bank balance	750

6   C

	$
Capital at 1.4.X7	6,500
Add profit (after drawings)	32,500
Less sales tax element	(70)
Capital at 31.3.X8	38,930

7   C   This will increase receivables but reduce cash.

8   D   Spread the net cost of the assets over their estimated useful life.

9   C

	Total $	Ordinary sales $	Private drawings $
Cost of sales	144,000	142,200	1,800
Mark-up:			
12% on cost	216	–	216
20% on sales (= 25% on cost)	35,550	35,550	
Sales	179,766	177,750	2,016

10   B $

      Net assets   31/12/X1
         2,000 + 500 + 300 − 50 + 200   2,950
      Net assets   31/12/X2
         2,500 + 100 + 50 − 600 − 100 + 250   2,200
      Decrease in net assets   750

      From the accounting equation

         Change in net assets =   Capital + profit − drawings

                          −750 =   Profit − drawings ($1,000)
                 −750 + 1,000   =   Profit
                          250   =   Profit

11   D   This is the accounting equation.

12   D   Reducing receivables will reduce current assets.

13   B   Drawings reduce capital, so they must be deducted.

20 Limited liability companies I

1   C   ($120,000 ÷ 800,000)

2   B   Preference dividend proposed during the current year, but paid in the following year.

3   A   Accumulated and undistributed profits of a company

4   C   ($100,000 × 10) × 5c + $50,000 (100,000/50c) × 5% = $50,000 ordinary + $2,500 preference.

5   B   The total will be $260,000, of which $60,000 will be credited to share premium.

6   C   Interest is classified as an expense; dividends are not.

7   D   This is correct because proposed dividends are current liabilities (if proposed before the year end).
    A   This is statutory reserve.
    B   Otherwise known as retained profits
    C   This is an unrealised reserve.

8   D   Correct, company will usually include this under distribution costs or administrative expenses.

    A   Incorrect, the contents of cost of sales are not defined by statute.

    B   Depreciation will be included under the relevant statutory expense heading. (eg office equipment
        depreciation will go into administrative expenses).

    C   Incorrect, net profit is calculated after interest.

9   A   Correct 15% × $500,000
    B   Incorrect, interest paid and accrued comprise the total expense for the year.
    C   Incorrect, only half a years interest is outstanding.
    D   Incorrect, this represents 18 months interest.

10	B		$
		Interim ordinary dividends 5c × 400,000	20,000
		Preference dividend (50,000 × $2 × 5%)/2	2,500
		Paid to date	22,500
		Final ordinary dividend 15c × 400,000	60,000
		Preference dividend (must be paid before final ordinary dividend)	2,500
			85,000

21 Limited liability companies II

1   D   SOCIE

2   B

Dividends

	$		$	
			35,000	b/d
Paid	50,000			
Balance c/d	45,000		60,000	Income statement
	95,000		95,000	

3   C   A reduction in the allowance for receivables reduces admin expenses and depreciation of machinery and the production director's salary would increase cost of sales.

4   D   This is a distribution of reserves.

5   A   Equity capital is owned by *ordinary* shareholders.

22 Incomplete records

1   A   We need to calculate credit sales first in order to calculate cash sales.

RECEIVABLES

	$		$
Bal b/f	2,100	Bank	24,290
∴ Credit sales	23,065	Bal c/f	875
	25,165		25,165

CASH

	$		$
Balance b/f	240	Expenses	1,850
Cash sales		Bank	9,300
(41,250 – 23,065)	18,185	∴ Theft	7,275
	18,425		18,425

2   A   Correct. 25% margin = $33\frac{1}{3}$% mark up. Cost of sales = 18,000 + 300,000 – 28,000 = 290,000. Mark up = 290,000 × $33\frac{1}{3}$% = $96,666, so sales = $386,666.

       B   Incorrect, you have applied the 25% margin to cost of sales.

	C	Incorrect because you have transposed the inventory figures in the calculation of cost of sales.
	D	Incorrect you have applied a mark up to purchases without the inventory adjustment.
3	D	Correct. $500,000 sales × 20% margin (25% mark up = 20% margin) = gross profit $100,000. Cost of sales = 400,000. Therefore closing inventory = 420,000 – 400,000 + 15,000 = $35,000.
	A	This is opening inventory.
	B	This is the difference between cost of sales and purchases ignoring inventory changes.
	C	You have incorrectly applied the mark up to sales.
4	A	Correct, 25% mark up = 20% margin so gross profit = 500,000 × 20% = 100,000. Therefore cost of sales = 400,000. Opening inventory was $10,000 and closing inventory was $20,000. Therefore cost of sales should have been 10,000 + 450,000 – 20,000 = 440,000. So losses = 440,000 – 400,000 = 40,000.
	B	Incorrect, you have applied the mark up % to sales.
	C	Incorrect, you have transposed opening and closing inventories in the calculation of theoretic cost of goods sold.
	D	Incorrect, you have forgotten to include the value of the remaining closing inventory and the original opening inventory.
5	D	Correct, calculate purchases in the period = $6,000 + $37,000 – $4,000 = $39,000. Sales $5,000 × margin 20% = $10,000, therefore cost of goods sold is calculated as $40,000.

Opening inventory 5,000 + purchases 39,000 =	$44,000 (theoretical cost of goods sold)
Cost of goods sold as calculated	$40,000
Inventory loss	$ 4,000

	A	Payables figures have been reversed in the calculation of purchases.
	B	Incorrect, payables have been ignored.
	C	Incorrect margin has been converted to a mark up in the calculation of cost of sales.

6   C

	$	$
Sales (10,000 × 220% × 50%)		11,000
Opening inventory	–	
Purchases	10,000	
	10,000	
Closing inventory	(5,000)	
Cost of goods sold		5,000
Gross profit		6,000
Less discount (5% × 11,000)		550
Net profit		5,450

7   B $(485) o/d + $1,450 + $2,400 – $1,710 ($1,800 × 95%) – $250 = $1,405 debit balance.

8   A

	$	$	
Sales		25,500	(100%)
Opening inventory	3,675		
Purchases	22,000		
Less closing inventory	(4,000)		
Cost of sales		21,675	(85%)
Gross profit		3,825	(15%)

9   B

	$	$	
Sales		25,500	(120%)
Opening inventory	5,250		
Purchases	26,000		
	31,250		
Closing inventory	(10,000)		
Cost of sales		21,250	(100%)
Gross profit		4,250	(20%)

10   C

	$	
Sales	21,950	(100%)
Less cost of sales	17,560	(80%)
Gross profit	4,390	(20%)

Receivables

B/d	3,050	21,000	Cash
Sales	21,950	4,000	C/d
	25,000	25,000	

And purchases are $21,950 × 80% = $17,560

11   D

	$	
Sales	36,400	(130%)
Less cost of sales	28,000	(100%)
Gross profit	8,400	
Less expenses	(14,000)	
Net loss	5,600	

12   A   Gross profit is $25,500 − $21,250 = $4,250, which is 16.67% of $25,500.

13   B

	$
Opening capital (balancing figure)	5,400
Capital introduced	9,800
Profits	8,000
	23,200
Drawings	(4,200)
	19,000

23 Income and expenditure accounts

1   D

		$	$
Subscriptions received in 20X5			790
Less: amounts relating to 20X4		38	
amounts relating to 20X6		80	
			118
Cash received relating to 20X5			672
Add: subs paid in 20X4 relating to 20X5		72	
20X5 subs still to be paid		48	
			120
			792

Alternatively, in ledger account format:

SUBSCRIPTIONS

	$		$
Balance b/f	38	Balance b/f	72
∴ Income and expenditure a/c	792	Cash	790
Balance c/f	80	Balance c/f	48
	910		910

2   B

	$
Subscriptions received in 20X5	1,024
Less amounts relating to 20X6	58
	966
Add subs paid in 20X4 relating to 20X5	14
	980

Alternatively, in ledger account format:

SUBSCRIPTIONS

	$		$
∴ Income and expenditure a/c	980	Balance b/f	14
Balance c/f	58	Bank	1,024
	1,038		1,038

3	C		$	$
		Balance at 1 January		3,780
		New enrolments (4 × $120)		480
				4,260
		Less release to income:		
		64 × $5	320	
		4 × $6	24	
				344
				3,916

4   A   Correct, the debit balance represents a deficit for the year.

      B   Incorrect, the debit balance represents a surplus of expenditure over income not an asset.

      C   Surpluses would be added, deficits are deducted.

      D   Incorrect the debit balance is not an asset.

5   D   Correct.

Subscriptions A/C

	$			$
Balance b/d				
20 × $20	400			
I&E subscriptions				
200 × $200	4,000	Bad debts		
Balance c/d		3 × $20	60	60
5 × $20	100	Bank		4,440
	4,500			4,500

      A   Incorrect, you have recorded the opening subscriptions in arrears as prepaid.

      B   Incorrect, you have carried down the closing prepaid subscriptions as arrears.

      C   Incorrect, you have posted bad debts to the incorrect side of the account.

6   A   Correct.

Subscriptions A/C

	$		$
Arrears b/f	700	Prepaid b/f	1,500
I&E a/c (balance)	13,000	Bank	14,200
Prepaid c/f	3,200	Arrears c/f	1,200
	16,800		16,900

      B   Incorrect, this is the amount of cash received and the receivables and prepayments have been ignored.

      C   Incorrect, you have transposed the opening balances.

      D   Incorrect, you have transposed the closing balances.

7	C	Correct, the club members will have to decide upon an appropriate period for release to revenue.
	A	Incorrect, this contravenes the accruals concept.
	B	Incorrect, these are liabilities not assets.
	D	Incorrect, these are liabilities of the club.

8 D Accumulated funds = net assets

9 C It is similar to a income statement and based on the accruals concept.

10 B

	$
Subscriptions received	12,500
Add subscriptions in arrears c/f	250
	12,750
Deduct: subscriptions in arrears b/f	800
subscriptions in advance c/f	400
	11,550

11 A These are funds received in advance so are treated as a liability, which diminishes over time.

12 B

SUBSCRIPTIONS ACCOUNT

		$			$
1.6.X7	Balance b/f	150	1.6.X7	Balance b/f	90
31.5.X8	Balance c/f	75		Bank	4,750
31.5.X8	Income and			Bad debts	40
	expenditure a/c	4,655*			
		4,880			4,880

* ie balancing figure

13 B Both are prepared for not-for-profit organisations.

14 C Income statements are also prepared for non-manufacturing businesses.

15 D It shows receipts and payments and is not based on accruals.

16 B

SUBSCRIPTIONS ACCOUNT

	$		$
Balance b/f	50	Balance b/f	75
Balance c/f	120	Bank	12,450
Income and expenditure a/c	12,355		
	12,525		12,525

24 Manufacturing accounts

1   B   The revenue cannot be recognised (or not) until 20X4 and the expenses should be in the same period.

2   A

	$	$
Raw materials		
Opening inventory	10,000	
Purchases	50,000	
Closing inventory	11,000	
Cost of raw materials		49,000
Direct wages		40,000
Prime cost		89,000
Production overheads		60,000
		149,000
Increase in work in progress		
4,000 – 2,000		(2,000)
Cost of goods manufactured		147,000

3   D   Because some of the WIP has been consumed to complete those goods.

4   A   Prime cost is direct material plus direct labour. There are no *direct* expenses.

5   D   See answer to 3 above.

6   B

	$
Purchase of raw materials	112,000
Decrease in inventory of raw materials	8,000
Carriage inwards	3,000
Raw materials used	123,000
Direct wages	42,000
Prime cost	165,000
Production overheads	27,000
Increase in WIP	(10,000)
Factory cost of finished goods	182,000

7

	$
Prime cost	56,000
Factory overheads	4,500
Opening WIP	6,200
Factory cost of	(57,000)
Therefore closing WIP is	9,700

8   D   Only *direct* costs are included in prime cost.

25 Audit I

1	A	A 'true and fair view' should enable users to make decisions based on the accounts.
2	C	The materiality concept applies here.
3	C	This is the *main* purpose.
4	D	This is part of their stewardship responsibilities.
5	C	External auditors are responsible to the shareholders.
6	A	A list of all the transactions in a period.
7	B	Co-operation between internal and external auditors can be valuable.
8	A	Correct. Small limited companies and unincorporated businesses or partnerships need not have an external audit.
	B	Incorrect, the auditor has rights and duties under the Act.
9	D	Correct, the responsibility rests with the external auditors (although they do rely on internal audit to carry out some of the work at times).
	A	Often in conjunction with the external auditors or a regulatory body.
	B	Studies of efficiency, economy and effectiveness of operations a re commonly carried out.
	C	Appraising and suggesting improvements to systems is a key task for internal audit.
10	B	The others are not internal audit functions.

26 Audit II

1	A	The stewardship function exercised by the directors.
2	C	They give users a 'true and fair' picture of the entity's financial position.
3	C	Correct. Unless the auditor is independent from the company, the work or reports will lack credibility in the eyes of users.
	A	This is an important attribute.
	B	This is vital and is developed by adequate training and appropriate experience.
	D	This is obviously desirable as an attribute but is not the most important.
4	B	Correct. Both should be professionals.
	A	Internal auditors report (ideally) to the chief executive whereas external auditors report to the shareholders.
	C	Internal auditors are employees whereas external auditors are appointed by the shareholders.
	D	Management will determine the objectives of internal auditors, the Companies Act determines the objectives of an external auditor.

5	B	Correct, the limits should be reviewed regularly.
	A	It is usual for different levels of authorisation to apply to monetary values or classes of transactions eg writing off an asset requires a high level of authority.
	C	Incorrect, all journal entries must be authorised to retain control.
	D	Incorrect, some form of authorisation is always possible eg supervision or printing out journal entries input for authorisation prior to processing.
6	C	Correct. Under the accruals concept, all dispatches in a period must be invoiced or accrued so they can be matched with costs of sale. Goods dispatched must be deducted from Inventory records.
	A	This is a completeness control.
	B	This is an accuracy control.
	D	Again, this is an accuracy control.
7	A	Correct. The impact of the weakness upon control risk should be evaluated, there may be an effective counter control which could mitigate the effects of the weakness.
	B	This should not be done until the facts are checked and cost effective solutions devised.
	C	The auditor should not enforce system changes, this is the role of management on receipt of recommendations from management.
	D	This is not an option!
8	B	Correct. This will not prevent fraud, the necessity to create fictitious bank details may make the fraud more difficult to carry out.
	A	An effective, but time consuming control to operate.
	C	This will be an effective aid to internal control.
	D	A common way of committing a payroll fraud is the manipulation of starting and leaving dates, independent authorisation will help to prevent this.
9	B	Correct. Usually this is a characteristic, the fraud is often not performed for personal gain.
	A	Management fraud can be simply the theft of assets, but usually it is more complex.
	C	Not all creative accounting devices are necessarily fraudulent.
	D	This is an example of a sophisticated type of fraud.
10	A	Correct. The problem with many computerised systems is that it is often difficult to ascertain the audit trail and identify mistakes. This is less likely in a manual system.
	D	Controls should be present in manual <u>and</u> computer systems.
11	A	Give an opinion on the financial statements.
12	B	Compliance with accounting standards.
13	D	Shareholders, although the directors may make the appointment on their behalf.

27 Statements of cash flows

1   A   B and D are statement of financial position items, C has not been deducted from operating profit.

2   B   Correct.

     A   Incorrect, Inventory increases reduce cash, receivable decreases improve cash flow.

     C   Incorrect, a payable increase improves cash flow.

     D   Incorrect, a payable increase improves cash flow.

3   A   Correct. $515,000 + $230,000 + $315,000 − $200,000.

     B   Incorrect, you have not included the rights issue.

     C   Incorrect, you have included interest paid which is reported under 'returns on investment and servicing finance'.

     D   Incorrect, you have not included the share premium received.

4   B   Correct ($1,200,000 − 100,000) − $50,000

     A   Incorrect, you have added depreciation which is reported under 'operating cash flows'.

     C   Incorrect ($1,200,000 − 100,000) + ($500,000) = $1,100,000 outflow but you have ignored receipts and also included the leased assets. The cash flow effect of these is the interest and capital repaid in the lease payments.

     D   Incorrect, you have included the non-current asset payable as a cash flow.

5   D

	Plant and machinery $	Motor vehicles $
Increase in cost (from non-current asset note)	1,100	2,100
Sold asset cost	2,000	
Total cost of assets acquired	3,100 +	2,100
	= 5,200	

6   A   The reduction in the overdraft is an increase in cash of $4,000.

       The reduction in short term investments (of $10,000) would be included in movement in liquid resources (not cash!)

7   C   The SOCIE shows the figure for dividends actually paid in the year.

28 Interpretation of accounts I

1   B

	Total $	Sales in first three quarters (9/15) $	Sales in final quarter (6/15) $
Sales	210,000	126,000	84,000
Mark-up:			
25% on cost (= 20% on sales)	16,800		16,800
20% on cost (=161/2 % on sales)	21,000	21,000	
	37,800		

| 2 | D | Cost of sales tells us what Inventory has been *used*. |

3   A   Transaction (a) would have no effect on working capital.

4   D   You will know this from question 2!

5   D $\$350 \times \dfrac{100}{140} = \$250$

6   A   Profit will be an addition to owner's capital (accounting equation!)

7   B   Inventory turnover = $\dfrac{\text{Cost of sales}}{\text{Average inventory}}$

Cost of sales $= 12 + 80 - 10 = 82$

Average Inventory $= \dfrac{12+10}{2} = 11$

$\therefore$ Inventory turnover $= \dfrac{82}{11} = 7.45$ times

8   C   Check this against question 4.

9   C   Non-current assets are not part of working capital but will give rise to a payable.

10   D   Purchases $= \$(32,500 - 6,000 + 3,800)$
$= \$30,300$

$\therefore$ Payables' payment period $= \dfrac{4,750}{30,300} \times 365 = 57$ days

29 Interpretation of accounts II

1   A   Gearing $= \dfrac{\text{debt}}{\text{debt} + \text{equity}} = \dfrac{75}{75+500} = 13\%$

2   C   Correct. This ratio is used to analyse the capital structure of a business.

3   C   Correct.

       A   Increased prices may result in reduced sales so asset turnover may fall.

       B   Selling price increases should increase margins.

       D   The effect of a price increase will be increased margins but reduced asset turnover, therefore effects on return on capital may be nil.

4   B   Correct. Current assets are normally inventory, receivables, bank. Current liabilities are normally payables, overdraft.

5   A   Correct. Inventory holding 2 months + 0.5 months in WIP + 3 months in finished goods inventory + 3 months receivable payment less 2 months credit from suppliers.

6	C	Correct, inventory, receivables, prepayments, cash.
	A	Cash is the most liquid so the order is reversed.
	B	Incorrect, cash is more liquid than receivables.
	D	Incorrect.

30 Ratios I

1   B

	%	$
Sales	100	2,400
Cost of sales	66 $^2/_3$	1,600
Gross profit	33 $^1/_3$	800
Expenses	28 $^1/_3$	680
Net profit	5	120

2   D

	%	$
Sales	150	180,000
COS	100	(120,000)
Gross profit	50	60,000

$$\therefore \text{Inventory turnover} = \frac{120,000}{(12,000+18,000)/2} = 8 \text{ times}$$

3   A $\dfrac{\text{Cost of sales}}{\text{Average inventory}} = \dfrac{\$24,500}{(4,000+6,000)\div 2} = 4.9 \text{ times}$

4   A   Long-term loans raise gearing, shareholders funds reduce it.

5   C   Current ratio is 2,900 : 1,100 = 2.6: 1 ie high

Acid test ratio is 1,000 : 1,100 = 0.9 ie acceptable

6   C

	$
Sales were	100,800
Cost of sales was	(72,000)
$\therefore$ Gross profit	28,800

$$\text{Gross profit mark up} = \frac{\$28,800}{\$72,000} \times 100 = 40\%$$

7   A   Current ratio = 1,390:420 = 3.3:1 (ie high)
Acid test = 420:420 = 1:1 (ie ideal)

8   C $\dfrac{\text{PBIT} \times 100}{\text{average capital}} = \dfrac{1,200 \times 100}{(11,200+11,800)/2} = 10.43\%$

9   C   Both receivables and payables will increase.

10   C   Long-term loans and preference shares as a percentage of total shareholders funds.

31 Ratios II

1   C   Correct.

       A   This is the often quoted 'ideal' quick ratio but many businesses (such as large supermarket chains) operate on much lower ratios.

       B   This is the 'ideal' current ratio which is often quoted – however it may be inappropriate for a particular business.

       D   Incorrect, unless matters are monitored, the business may suddenly arrive at a funding crisis.

2   B   Correct. Increasing the bank overdraft will increase payables, which will lower the current ratio.
       A   If inventory turnover decreases, inventory levels increase and relatively the current ratio will rise.
       C   This will reduce payables and will therefore increase the current ratio.
       D   This will increase receivables and the current ratio is likely to increase.

3   D   Correct: $\dfrac{2.5+0.5}{2.5+1.5+0.5+2.2+0.2} \times \dfrac{100}{1} = 44\%$

       A   This is debt ÷ ordinary shares + premium.

       B   This is the debt/equity ratio ie. $\dfrac{2.5+0.5}{2.2+1.5+0.2} = 77\%$

       C   You have ignored the effect of the preference shares as prior charge capital.

4   B   Return on capital employed can be measured in many ways. Your examiner has stated that capital employed includes long term loans.

$$\text{So ROCE} = \frac{\text{Profit before interest and tax}}{\text{Capital} + \text{reserves} + \text{debentures}} \times 100\%$$

$$= \frac{\$2,500}{3,400+3,000} \times 100\%$$

$$= \frac{\$2,500}{6,400} = 39\%$$

       C   which is $\dfrac{\text{Profit before tax}}{\text{Capital and reserves}} = \dfrac{\$2,200}{3,400} \times 100\%$ is sometimes used to calculate ROCE but is excluded by your examiner as it ignores long term debt, which is a source of capital employed.

5   B   Asset turnover is $\dfrac{\text{Turnover}}{\text{Capital employed}} = \dfrac{\$12,000}{\$3,400+3,000} = \dfrac{\$12,000}{\$6,400} = 1.875$ times

6   D   Gross profit margin $= \dfrac{\text{Gross profit}}{\text{turnover}} \times 100\% = \dfrac{\$5,000}{\$12,000} \times 100\%$

$$= 42\%$$

Net profit margin $= \dfrac{\text{Profit before interest and tax}}{\text{turnover}} \times 100\% = \dfrac{\$2,500}{12,000}$

$$= 21\%$$

7   C   Inventory days are $\dfrac{\text{Inventory}}{\text{Cost of sales}} \times 365 = \dfrac{1,200}{7,000} \times 365$

$$= 62 \text{ days}$$

Receivable days are $\dfrac{\text{Receivables}}{\text{turnover}} \times 365 = \dfrac{1,700}{12,000} \times 365$

$$= 52 \text{ days}$$

8   A   The cash cycle is inventory days + receivable days less payable days:

Inventory days $= \dfrac{\text{Inventory}}{\text{Cost of sales}} \times 365 = 62 \text{ days}$

Receivable days $= \dfrac{\text{Receivables}}{\text{turnover}} \times 365 = 52 \text{ days}$

Payable days $= \dfrac{\text{Payables}}{\text{Cost of sales}} \times 365 = \underline{(78 \text{ days})}$

Cash cycle is $\underline{36 \text{ days}}$

9   B   Current ratio $= \dfrac{\text{Current assets}}{\text{Current liabilities}} = \dfrac{\$3,200}{\$1,500} = 2.13$

Gearing ratio $= \dfrac{\text{Loan capital + preference shares}}{\text{Total capital employed}} = \dfrac{3,000 + 400}{2,000 + 400 + 1,000 + 3,000} = 53\%$

10   B   Payable days $= \dfrac{\text{Payables}}{\text{Cost of sales}} \times 365$

$$= \dfrac{1,500}{7,000} \times 365$$

$$= 78 \text{ days}$$

Answers to
Objective test questions

1 Ledger accounting and books of prime entry I

1

	Dr	Cr
	$	$
Discount allowed	32	
Receivables control account (PQ)		32

Sale price $800 – (20% × 800) = $640
Cash discount $640 × 5% = $32

2 The gross profit for March 20X8 is $22,000

Reconstruction of the trading account

	$	$
Sales		40,000
Returns inwards		(2,000)
		38,000
Opening inventory	3,000	
Purchases	20,000	
Returns outwards	(4,000)	
Closing inventory	(3,000)	
		(16,000)
Gross profit		22,000

3 Diesel fuel charge = $87,700

Diesel fuel payable account		*Cost of fuel used*	
	$		$
Balance b/fwd	(1,700)	Opening inventory	12,500
Payments	85,400	Purchases	85,000
Balance c/fwd	1,300	Closing inventory	(9,800)
Purchases	85,000	Transfer to I/S	87,700

4 A decrease in **receivables** and **decreases** the profit for the year.

5 Amounts required to restore imprest = $80.70

	$
Stationery	14.10
Travel	25.50
Refreshments	12.90
Sundry payables ($24 × 1.175)	28.20
	80.70

6   Telephone charge = $2,185

TELEPHONE ACCOUNT

		$			$
Prepayment b/f (2/3 × $90)		60	Accrual b/f		80
Bills paid		2,145	I/S account		2,185
Accrual c/f		120	Prepayment c/f (2/3 × $90)		60
		2,325			2,325

7   Rent payable = $6,000.

RENT PAYABLE ACCOUNT

		$			$
1.10.X5	Bal b/fwd	1,000	30.9.X6	Charge to I/S a/c	6,000
30.11.X5	Bank	1,500	30.9.X6	Rent prepaid c/fwd	
29.2.X6	Bank	1,500		(1500 × 2/3)	1,000
31.5.X6	Bank	1,500			
31.8.X6	Bank	1,500			
		7,000			7,000
1.10.X6	Rent prepaid b/fwd	1,000			

Alternatively, as you are told that the rent is $6,000 per annum and there has been no increase or decrease this must be the annual charge.

8   Electricity charge = $5,000.

ELECTRICITY ACCOUNT

		$			$
5.11.X5	Bank	1,000	1.10.X5	Bal b/fwd	800
10.2.X6	Bank	1,300	30.9.X6	Charge to I/S a/c	5,000
8.5.X6	Bank	1,500			
7.8.X6	Bank	1,100			
30.9.X6	Accrual c/fwd	900			
		5,800			5,800
			1.10.X6	Balance b/fwd	900

9   Interest receivable = $850.

INTEREST RECEIVABLE ACCOUNT

		$			$
1.10.X5	Bal b/fwd	300	2.10.X5	Bank	250
30.9.X6	Transfer to I/S a/c	850	3.4.X6	Bank	600
			30.9.X6	Accrual c/fwd	300
		1,150			1,150
1.10.X6	Balance b/fwd	300			

10 Allowance for receivables = $1,450 charge to income statement.

ALLOWANCE FOR RECEIVABLES

		$			$
30.9.X6	Bal c/fwd		1.10.X5	Bal b/fwd	4,800
	(125,000 × 5%)	6,250	30.9.X6	Charge to I/S a/c	1,450
		6,250			6,250
			1.10.X6	Balance b/fwd	6,250

2 Ledger accounting and books of prime entry II

1

Book of original entry	Debit entries		Credit entries	
	Account	$	Account	$
Purchase day book	Purchases	18,000		
	Sales tax	3,150	J Burgess	21,150

2

Book of original entry	Debit entries		Credit entries	
	Account	$	Account	$
Cash book	P Barton	14,000	Bank	13,720
			Discount received	280

3

Book of original entry	Debit entries		Credit entries	
	Account	$	Account	$
Journal	Office equipment	2,500	J Smithers	2,500

4

Book of original entry	Debit entries		Credit entries	
	Account	$	Account	$
Journal	Bad debts	500	A Scholes	500

5

Book of original entry	Debit entries		Credit entries	
	Account	$	Account	$
Returns inwards day book	Returns inward	400	J Lockley	470
	Sales tax	70		

6

Book of original entry	Debit entries		Credit entries	
	Account	$	Account	$
Journal	Motor vehicle	1,325	A Jackson	1,400
	Motor expenses	75		

7   Rates payable = $1,830

RATES ACCOUNT

	$		$
1.5.X1 Balance b/f (1,800 × 11/12)	1,650	30.4.X2 Income statement	1,830
1.4.X2 Rates paid	2,160	30.4.X2 Balance c/f (2,160 × 11/12)	1,980
	3,810		3,810

8   Rent payable = $1,300

RENT ACCOUNT

	$		$
1.5.X1 Rent paid	300	1.5.X1 Balance b/f	300
1.8.X1 Rent paid	300		
1.11. X1 Rent paid	300		
1.2.X2 Rent paid	300		
30.4/X2 Balance c/f (1,600/4)	400	30.4.X2 Income statement	1,300
	1,600		1,600

An alternative calculation is:

	$
Rent payable 1.5.X1 to 31.1.X2 (1,200 × 9/12)	900
Rent payable 1.2.X2 to 30.4.X2 (1,600 × 3/12)	400
Total rent payable	1,300

3 Conceptual and regulatory framework

1   1.   Employees
     2.   The government

2   1.   Going concern
     2.   Accruals

3   Prudence

4

	Capital expenditure	Revenue expenditure
Redecoration of factory		*
New engine for machinery	*	
Cleaning of factory		*
Purchase of delivery van	*	

5   The accruals concept

6   False. Accounting standards are issued by the Accounting Standards Board.

4 Non-current assets

1   Loss on disposal = $87

	$
$9,000 \times 0.7 \times 0.7 \times 0.7 =$	3,087 (NBV)
Proceeds of sale	(3,000)
Loss on disposal	87

As this is the reducing balance method, the residual value is included in the 30% rate.

2   Going concern concept.

3   Loss on disposal = $360

	$
NBV ($5,000 $\times$ 0.8 $\times$ 0.8 $\times$ 0.8)*	2,560
Proceeds	(2,200)
Loss on disposal	360

* Remember this is the reducing balance method, the residual value is included in the 20% rate.

4   … over the accounting periods ….

5   Profit on sale = $1,500

	$
NBV ($64,000 $\times$ 0.5 $\times$ 0.5 $\times$ 0.5 $\times$ 0.5)	4,000
Proceeds	(5,500)
Profit	1,500

As this is the reducing balance method, the residual value is included in the 50% rate.

6   20X2 depreciation charge = $450

$$\text{Annual depreciation} = \frac{\text{Cost minus residual value}}{\text{Estimated life}}$$

$$\text{Annual depreciation} = \frac{\$1,800 - \$0}{4 \text{ years}}$$

20X2 depreciation = $450

7   20X2 depreciation charge = $432

	$	
Cost at 1.1.20X1	1,800	
Depreciation 20X1	1,080	60% $\times$ $1,800
Book value 1.1.20X2	720	
Depreciation 20X2	432	60% $\times$ $720
Book value 1.1.20X3	288	

5 Inventories

1   1.   FIFO (first in, first out)
     2.   Average cost

2   Gross profit: FIFO $400 + adjustment opening inventory ($200 – $180) – adjustment closing inventory ($270 – $300) = $390,000

3   FIFO $\dfrac{(200 + 300)/2}{600} \times 365$ days = 152 days

4   LIFO $\dfrac{(180 + 270)/2}{610} \times 365$ days = 135 days (But remember that IAS 2 does not allow LIFO)

6 Bank reconciliations

1   Corrected cash book balance = $1,681 debit.

CASH BOOK

20X8		$	20X8		$
Dec 31	Balance b/d	1,793	Dec 31	Bank charges	18
Dec 31	Dividend	26	Dec 31	Standing order	32
			Dec 31	Direct debit	88
				Balance c/d	1,681
		1,819			1,819

2   Add **unrecorded lodgements** of $232

     Deduct **unpresented cheques** of $108

BANK RECONCILIATION AS AT 31 DECEMBER 20X8

	$	$
Balance per bank statement		1,557
Add unrecorded lodgements:		
V Owen	98	
K Walters	134	
		232
Less unpresented cheques:		
B Oliver (869)	71	
L Philips (872)	37	
		(108)
Balance per cash book (corrected)		1,681

3   Cash book balance = $2,098 overdrawn

CASH BOOK

		$			$
31.5.X3	Balance b/d	873	31.5.X3	Bank charges	630
	Error $(936 – 693)	243		Standing orders	2,584
31.5.X3	Balance c/d	2,098			
		3,214			3,214
			1.6.X3	Balance b/d	2,098

4   Balance per bank statement = $974 (in credit)

BANK RECONCILIATION

	$
Balance per cash book	(901)
Outstanding lodgements	(593)
Unpresented cheques	2,468
Balance per bank statement	974

7 Control accounts, sales tax and payroll

1

	$
36 × $3.50	126.00
Employer's NI	12.60
Gross wages cost (I/S account)	138.60
36 × $3.50	126.00
Tax (($126 – 75) × 20%)	(10.20)
Employees' NI	(8.82)
Paid to employee	106.98

2    $901

Cash discounts allowed should be credited. So a debit of $901 would result in an error of $1,802 between the ledger and the control account.

3

		$
Wages paid		12,450
Employee deductions	– tax	2,480
	– NI	1,350
	– pension	900
Gross wages		17,180

4   X is a receivable of Y or X owes Y.

5   Balance at 1 June 20X2 = $13,000

RECEIVABLES CONTROL ACCOUNT

	$		$
Opening balance (bal fig)	13,000	Sales returns	6,200
Sales	164,500	Bank	155,300
		Discounts allowed	5,100
		Bad debts written off	2,600
		Closing balance	8,300
	177,500		177,500

6   Closing balance = $23,045

PAYABLES CONTROL ACCOUNT

	$		$
Returns outwards	9,045	Opening balance	17,600
Discounts received	2,070	Purchases	227,540
Bank	210,040		
Contra	940		
Closing balance	23,045		
	245,140		245,140

8 Correction of errors and suspense accounts

1   Credit

The entries are Dr Expenses $200, Cr Bank $210.

2   The balance on the current account is $9,600.

SUSPENSE ACCOUNT

	$		$
		Balance b/d	14,000
Discounts received	14,000	Discounts allowed	6,000
Current a/c – partner's wife	9,600	Payables control a/c	3,600
	23,600		23,600

3

		$	$
DR	Receivable	300	
CR	Payable		300

4

		$	$
DR	Heat & light	300	
CR	Suspense account		300

5

		$	$
DR	G Gordon	800	
CR	G Goldman		800

6

		$	$
DR	Insurance prepayment	500	
CR	Suspense account		500

7

		$	$
DR	Purchase returns	700	
CR	Suspense account		700

8 Corrected profit = $8,750

	$
First draft profit	9,750
Adjustment re heat and light	(300)
Adjustment re purchase returns	(700)
Revised net profit	8,750

9 Receivable = $1,800 ($1,500 + $300)

10 Prepayments = $900 ($400 + $500)

11 Payables = $2,000 ($1,700 + $300)

9 Final accounts and audit I

1 Gross Profit = $55,141

	$	$
Sales		138,078
Opening inventory	11,927	
Purchases (W)	84,561	
	96,488	
Less closing inventory	13,551	
Cost of goods sold		82,937
Gross profit		55,141

Purchases

	$
Per trial balance	82,350
Add carriage inwards	2,211
Per I/S a/c	84,561

2 Rent and insurance = $5,952

	$
Per trial balance	6,622
Add: rent accrual	210
Less: insurance prepayment	(880)
	5,952

3 Summarised statement of financial position at 31 May 20X6

	$	$
Non-current assets (58,000 – (19,000 + 15% × 58,000))		30,300
Current assets (W)	27,560	
Current liabilities (6,471 + 210)	(6,681)	
Net current assets		20,879
Total assets less current liabilities		51,179

WORKING

	$
Inventory	13,551
Receivables (12,120 – 130 – 40)	11,950
Prepayment	880
Cash in hand	177
Cash at bank	1,002
	27,560

4 Subscription income = $4,655.

MEMBERSHIP SUBSCRIPTIONS

	$		$
Bal b/f	200	Bal b/f	90
∴ I&E	4,655	Received	4,800
Subs paid in advance c/f	85	Subs in arrears c/f	50
	4,940		4,940

5 The accumulated fund represents the book value of net assets in a not-for-profit organisation.

6 Cash sales = $10,850

CASH BOOK

	Cash $		Cash $
Balance b/d	55	Drawings (52 × $50)	2,600
Cash takings (balancing figure)	10,850	Petrol (52 × $10)	520
		Sundry expenses	24
		Repairs to canopy	201
		Takings banked (contra entry)	7,521
		Balance c/d	39
	10,905		10,905
Balance b/d	39		

7   Credit sales = $1,650.

RECEIVABLES

	$		$
Balance b/d	170	Cash	1,500
Credit sales - balancing figure	1,650	Balance c/d	320
	1,820		1,820

8   Purchases = $7,600

PAYABLES

	$		$
Bank	7,777	Balance b/d	230
Balance c/d	233	Purchases (balancing figure)	7,780
	8,010		8,010

Goods taken as drawings

	$
Selling price (100%)	300
Gross profit (40%)	120
Cost (60%)	180

Therefore, purchases taken to the trading account = $7,780 – $180 = $7,600.

9   New van depreciation charge = $1,000

The bank statement shows that the cash paid for the new van was $3,200. Since there was a part exchange of $1,800 on the old van, the cost of the new van must be $5,000 with first year depreciation (20%) $1,000.

10   Profit on disposal = $1,300.

	$		$
Van at cost	3,000	Provision for depreciation at	
Profit on disposal	1,300	date of sale	2,500
		Asset account (trade in value for	
		new van)	1,800
	4,300		4,300

11   Other expenses = $2,300

	$	$
Expenses:		
Rent	970	
Repairs to canopy	201	
Van running expenses (520 + 80 + 323)	923	
Sundry expenses (24 + 31)	55	
Bank interest	47	
Accounting fees	75	
Bad debts	29	
		2,300

10 Final accounts and audit II

1   Closing inventory = $500.

	$
Sales (100%)	15,000
Gross profit (30%)	4,500
Cost of goods sold (70%)	10,500
Opening inventory	1,000
Purchases (from previous question)	10,000
	11,000
Cost of goods sold	10,500
Closing inventory (balancing figure)	500

2   Factory cost of goods completed = $96,800.

	$
Purchases of raw materials	56,000
Increase in inventories of raw materials	(1,700)
Direct wages	21,000
Carriage inwards	2,500
Production overheads	14,000
Decrease in work-in-progress	5,000
Factory cost of sales	96,800

Returns inwards are returns of sales and so do not form part of the factory cost of goods.

3   Prime cost = $115,000

	$
Opening inventory	25,000
Purchases	80,000
	105,000
Less: closing inventory	(24,000)
Raw materials used	81,000
Direct wages	34,000
Prime cost	115,000

4   Total depreciation charge = $9,000

	Non-current assets at cost	Net book value	Accumulated depreciation
	$	$	$
At 31 December 20X4	60,000	39,000	21,000
At 31 December 20X5	90,000	60,000	30,000
Depreciation charge for the year			9,000

5   The factory cost of goods completed during the year was $682,000

	$
Prime cost	720,000
Factory overheads	72,000
Add: Opening work in progress	240,000
Less: Closing work in progress	(350,000)
Factory cost of goods completed	682,000

6   The gross profit for the year is $94,000

	$
Opening inventory of raw materials	18,000
Purchases	163,000
	181,000
Less: closing inventory of raw materials	(21,000)
Raw materials used	160,000
Manufacturing expenses	115,000
Factory cost of goods produced	275,000

	$	$
Sales		365,000
Less: Cost of goods sold		
Opening finished goods inventory	34,000	
Factory cost of goods produced	275,000	
	309,000	
Less: Closing inventory of finished goods	(38,000)	
		271,000
Gross profit		94,000

7   Increase in cash and bank balances = $13,150

	$
Profit for the year	18,750
Add back depreciation	1,250
	20,000
Purchase of non-current assets	(8,000)
Increase in receivables	(1,000)
Decrease in inventories	1,800
Increase in payables	350
∴ Increase in cash and bank	13,150

11 Interpretation of accounts I

1   Retained profit = $264,000

	$	$
Profit before tax		445,000
Tax		111,000
Profit after tax		334,000
Transfer to general reserve	30,000	
Interim dividend	40,000	
		70,000
Retained profit		264,000

2   Total payables = $128,000

	$
Trade payables and accruals	17,000
Corporation tax	111,000
	128,000

3   Amended retained profits reserve = $69,000

	$
Draft retained profits reserve	84,000
Adjustment for closing inventory	(10,000)
Transfer to general reserve	(5,000)
	69,000

	$
4 Share capital (200,000 + 50,000)	250,000
5 Share premium (40,000 + 30,000)	70,000
6 General reserve (20,000 + 5,000)	25,000

7   Mark up = 51.67%

	$
Sales ($130,000 × 140%)	182,000
Cost of sales (2 × $60,000)	120,000
Gross profit	62,000

$$\text{Mark up} = \frac{62,000}{120,000} = 51.67\%$$

8   Mark up = 60%

$$
\begin{array}{lr}
 & \$ \\
\text{Sales (160\% of cost of sales)} & 240,000 \\
\text{Cost of sales (\$240,000/1.6)} & 150,000 \\
\text{Gross profit} & 90,000 \\
\end{array}
$$

Mark up $= \dfrac{90,000}{150,000} = 60\%$

9   Gearing $= \dfrac{\text{Prior charge capital}}{\text{Total capital}} \times 100\%$

$= \dfrac{10}{48}$

$= 20.8\%$

10   ROCE $= \dfrac{\text{Profit before interest and tax}}{\text{Average capital employed}} \times 100\%$

$= \dfrac{5.6(\text{W1})}{46.25(\text{W2})} \times 100\%$

$= 12.1\%$

Workings

1   *Profit before interest and tax*

	$m
Profit before interest and tax (bal. fig.)	5.6
Interest (10 × 6%)	0.6
Tax	1.0
Profit after tax	4.0

2   *Average capital employed*

	$m
Capital at end of year	48.0
Retained profit (4 – 0.5)	3.5
Capital at start of year	44.5

∴ Average capital employed $= \dfrac{48+44.5}{2} = \$46.25\text{m}$

12 Interpretation of accounts II

1   The gross profit margin is

	20X4	20X5
2,600/14,400	18.1%	
4,400/17,000		25.9%

2   The net profit margin is

	20X4	20X5
1,400/14,400	9.7%	
2,400/17,000		14.1%

3   The return on capital employed is

	20X4	20X5
(2,600 – 1,000)/6,700	23.9%	
2,400/5,720		42.0%

4   The acid test ratio is

	20X4	20X5
(2,000 + 2,400)/1,500	2.9:1	
(1,600 + 820)/2,700		0.9:1

5   The asset turnover is

	20X4	20X5
14,400/6,700	2.1 times	
17,000/5,720		3.0 times

6   The inventory turnover period in days is

	20X4	20X5
1,300/11,800 × 365	40 days	
2,000/12,600 × 365		58 days

7   The gearing ratio is

	20X4	20X5
2,600/6,700 × 100	38.9 %	0 %

Mock assessments

CIMA
Paper C2 (Certificate)
Fundamentals of
Financial Accounting

Mock Assessment 1

Question Paper	
Time allowed	*2 hours*
Answer ALL the questions	

**DO NOT OPEN THIS PAPER UNTIL YOU ARE READY TO START UNDER
EXAMINATION CONDITIONS**

Answer ALL 50 questions

1   An imprest system is

    A   Accounting computer software
    B   An audit process
    C   Automatic agreement of the cash book and bank statement
    D   A method of controlling petty cash

2   Which ONE of the following is correct?

    A   All limited companies are required by law to have an external audit
    B   Only public limited companies are required by law to have an external audit
    C   Only limited companies above a certain size are required by law to have an external audit
    D   An external audit for a limited company is voluntary

3   At 31 March 20X1, accrued rent payable was $300. During the year ended 31 March 20X2, rent paid was $4,000, including an invoice for $1,200 for the quarter ended 30 April 20X2. What is the income statement charge for rent payable for the year ended 31 March 20X2?

    A $3,300
    B $3,900
    C $4,100
    D $4,700

4   The responsibility for internal control rests with

    A   The internal auditors
    B   The external auditors
    C   The shareholders
    D   The directors

5   The annual insurance premium for S for the period 1 July 20X1 to 30 June 20X2 is $13,200, which is 10% more than the previous year. Insurance premiums are paid on 1 July.

    What is the income statement charge for the year ended 31 December 20X1?

    A $11,800
    B $12,540
    C $12,600
    D $13,200

6   A bank reconciliation showed the following differences between the bank statement and the cash book.

   Unpresented cheques of $750
   Outstanding deposits of $500
   Bank charges of $100

   If the balance on the bank statement is $1,000 overdrawn, what is the balance in the cash book before any adjustments?

$	

   Debit/credit

---

7   Which ONE of the following expenses should be included in prime cost in a manufacturing account?

   A   Repairs to factory machinery
   B   Direct production wages
   C   Office salaries
   D   Factory insurance

---

8   The entries in a receivables control account are:

	$
Sales	250,000
Bank	225,000
Returns	2,500
Bad debts	3,000
Returned unpaid cheque	3,500
Contra purchase ledger account	4,000

   What is the balance on the receivables control account? ....

---

9   A has an item in inventory which cost $1,000 and can be sold for $1,200. However, before it can be sold, it will require to be modified at a cost of $150. The expected selling costs of the item are an additional $100.

   How should this item be valued in inventory?

   A $950
   B $1,000
   C $1,050
   D $1,100

---

10   A 'value for money' audit is:

   A   An external audit with limited scope.
   B   A review of expenditure to ensure effectiveness, efficiency and economy.
   C   A voluntary audit by an unregistered auditor.
   D   None of these.

11   Which ONE of the following statements regarding a non-current assets register is NOT correct?

      A   A non-current assets register enables reconciliation to be made with the nominal ledger
      B   A non-current assets register enables depreciation charges to be posted to the nominal ledger
      C   A non-current assets register agrees with the non-current asset nominal ledger account
      D   A non-current assets register records the physical location of an asset

12   B purchased a machine for $120,000 on 1 October 20X1. The estimated useful life is 4 years with a residual value of $4,000. B uses the straight-line method for depreciation and charges depreciation on a monthly basis.

      What is the charge for depreciation for the year ended 31 December 20X1?

      A $7,250
      B $7,500
      C $29,000
      D $30,000

13   In the quarter ended 31 March 20X2, C had sales taxable outputs, net of sales tax, of $90,000 and taxable inputs, net of sales tax, of $72,000.

      If the rate of sales tax is 10%, how much sales tax is due?

      A $1,800 receivable
      B $2,000 receivable
      C $1,800 payable
      D $2,000 payable

14   Which of the following statements concerning a 'true and fair view' is correct?

      A   True and fair has a precise definition which is universally accepted
      B   There can only be one true and fair view of a company's financial statements
      C   True and fair means the financial statements are correct
      D   True and fair is mainly determined by compliance with generally accepted accounting practice

15   The M Club discloses the following note to its Income and Expenditure Account:

      'Subscriptions in arrears are accounted for when received; subscriptions in advance are accounted for on a matching basis.'

      At 31 March 20X1, there were subscriptions owing of $1,000 and subscriptions in advance of $500. During the year ended 31 March 20X2, subscriptions of $10,000 were received, including subscriptions relating to the previous year of $800 and subscriptions in advance of $600.

      What amount should be included for subscriptions in the year ended 31 March 20X2?

      A $8,100
      B $8,900
      C $9,100
      D $9,900

16   The total cost of salaries charged to the income statement is:

    A   The total gross salaries plus employer's national insurance contributions
    B   The total gross salaries
    C   The total net salaries
    D   The total net salaries plus employer's national insurance contributions

17   The segregation of duties is

    A   Delegation of duties by a manager
    B   Two staff sharing one job
    C   A feature of internal control
    D   All of the above

18   The net profit percentage in a company is 12% and the asset turnover ratio is 2.

    What is the return on capital employed? ....

19   Which of the following are used in a coding system for accounting transactions?

    A   Department code
    B   Nominal ledger code
    C   Product code
    D   All of the above

20   APM provides the following note to non-current assets in its statement of financial position.

Plant and machinery

	Cost $'000	Depreciation $'000	Net book value $'000
Opening balance	25	12	13
Additions/charge	15	4	11
Disposals	(10)	(8)	(2)
Closing balance	30	8	22

The additional machinery was purchased for cash. A machine was sold at a profit of $2,000.

What is the net cash outflow for plant and machinery?

    A $9,000
    B $11,000
    C $13,000
    D $15,000

21   Which of the following errors will cause the trial balance totals to be unequal?

    A   Errors of transposition
    B   Errors of omission
    C   Errors of principle
    D   All of the above

22 Which ONE of the following is a record of prime entry?

A   The nominal ledger
B   The sales ledger
C   The trial balance
D   The sales day book

23 P is a sole proprietor whose accounting records are incomplete. All the sales are cash sales and during the year $50,000 was banked, including $5,000 from the sale of a business car. He paid $12,000 wages in cash from the till and withdrew $2,000 per month as drawings. The cash in the till at the beginning and end of the year was $300 and $400 respectively.

What were the sales for the year?

A $80,900
B $81,000
C $81,100
D $86,100

24 Which of the following is NOT helpful in detecting an error?

A   A bank reconciliation
B   A sales ledger control account
C   An imprest system
D   A suspense account

25 Which ONE of the following is an appropriation by a limited liability company?

A   Directors' salaries
B   Dividends
C   Donation to a charity
D   Loan interest

26 At the year end of SED in December 20X0, a journal entry was raised to accrue for utility expenses of $3,600. This journal entry was reversed in January 20X1. During the year ended December 20X1, $30,000 was paid for utility expenses, of which $4,000 was prepaid at the year end.

The charge to the income statement for utility expenses for the year ended December 20X1 was

$ ....

27 Z's cash book shows a credit balance of $2,200. A comparison with the bank statement showed the following:

(i)   unpresented cheques totalling $600;

(ii)   receipts of $1,200 not yet cleared by the bank;

(iii)   bank charges of $300 not entered in the cash book;

(iv)   a cheque from a customer for $400, which had been entered in the cash book when received, has now been returned by the bank as 'dishonoured'.

The overdraft balance on Z's bank statement is $ ....

The following data relates to questions 28 and 29

On the first day of Month 1, a business had prepaid insurance of $10,000. On the first day of Month 8, it paid in full the annual insurance invoice of $36,000, to cover the following year.

28   The amount charged in the income statement for insurance for the year is $ ....

29   The amount shown in the statement of financial position at the year end is $ ....

30   SSG bought a machine for $40,000 in January 19W8. The machine had an expected useful life of six years and an expected residual value of $10,000. The machine was depreciated on the straight-line basis. In December 20X1, the machine was sold for $15,000. The company has a policy in its internal accounts of combining the depreciation charge with the profit or loss on disposal of assets.

The total amount of depreciation and profit/loss charged to the internal income statement over the life of the machine was $ ....

31   DEF has a supplier, M, and the balance on M's purchase ledger account at 31 July 20X2 was a credit balance of $2,000. On 5 August 20X2, DEF received the July statement from M showing a balance due of $3,000. The purchase ledger supervisor investigates the difference and discovers that:

(i)   an invoice for $2,000 from M dated 31 July was not entered in the purchase ledger account until 3 August 20X2, but appears on M's July statement.

(ii)   a cheque for $600 sent from DEF to M on 25 July 20X2 in payment of a July invoice does not appear on M's July statement. This cheque was presented by M on 31 July 20X2.

The purchase ledger supervisor at DEF contacts the sales ledger supervisor at M and correctly says that there is a difference between the ledger accounts of $ ....

32   On 1 October 20X2, the receivables' balance at G was $80,000. A summary of the transactions in the month of October is set out below.

	$
Cheques received	100,000
Contra payables	6,000
Sales	90,000
Returns inwards	4,000
Discounts allowed	10,000

The receivables' balance at 31 October was $ ....

33   SAD paid $240,000 in net wages to its employees in August 20X2. Employees' tax was $24,000, employees' national insurance was $12,000 and employer's national insurance was $14,000. Employees had contributed $6,000 to a pension scheme and had voluntarily asked for $3,000 to be deducted for charitable giving.

The amount to be charged to the income statement in August 20X2 for wages is $ ....

---

34   At the beginning of Period 6, XYZ had opening inventory of 20 units of product X valued at $4.00 each. During Period 6, the following inventory movements occurred:

Day 5   Sold 15 items for $5.00 each
Day 10   Bought 8 items for $6.00 each
Day 14   Sold 12 items for $7.00 each

Using the FIFO method of inventory valuation, the closing inventory at the end of Period 6 was

$ ....

The following data relates to questions 35 to 37

The accounts for SPA are set out below.

Income statement for the year ended 30 November 20X2

	$'000	$'000
Turnover		5,000
Opening inventory	200	
Purchases	3,100	
Closing inventory	(300)	
Cost of sales		(3,000)
Gross profit		2,000
Operating expenses		(500)
Operating profit		1,500

Statement of financial position at 30 November 20X2

	$'000	$'000
Non-current assets		3,000
Current assets		
Inventory	300	
Receivables	900	
Bank	50	
		1,250
		4,250
Share capital		2,000
Retained profits		2,000
		4,000
Current liabilities		
Trade payables		250
		4,250

35   The return on capital employed in SPA is ....

36   The non-current asset turnover ratio in SPA is ....

37   The quick ratio (acid test ratio) in SPA is ....

38   Tanwir commenced his business on 1 October 20X9, with capital in the bank of $20,000. During his first
      month of trading, his transactions were as follows.

1 October	Purchase inventories for $3,500 on credit from A Jones
3 October	Paid $1,200 rental of premises, by cheque
5 October	Paid $5,000 for office equipment, by cheque
10 October	Sold goods costing $1,000 for $1,750, on credit to P Duncan
15 October	Returned inventories costing $500 to A Jones
18 October	Purchased inventories for $2,400 on credit from A Jones
25 October	Paid A Jones for the net purchases of 1 October, by cheque
28 October	P Duncan paid $500 on account, by cheque

      The balance on the account of A Jones at 31 October 20X9 was $ ....

The following data relates to questions 39 and 40

During his first year of trading, Tanwir brings his private car, valued at $6,000 into the business as well as his initial
$20,000 of capital. The business made a net profit of $17,500 for the year, after deducting $650 for petrol which
was paid out of his private funds. He has drawn $5,000 out of the business bank account for himself, as well as
paying his home telephone bill of $450 from business funds.

39   Tanwir's capital at the end of his first year of trading was $ ....

40   State the accounting concept which has governed the treatment of the items which make up Tanwir's capital
      at the end of the year. ....

41   A business is normally said to have earned revenue when

      A   cash has been received
      B   a customer is legally obliged to pay for goods delivered or services rendered
      C   an order has been placed
      D   goods have been manufactured and placed in inventory

42   The role of the internal auditors is best described as

      A   auditing the financial accounts
      B   supporting the work of the external auditors
      C   reporting to management on the accounting systems
      D   ensuring value for money

43 The following information relates to C at 30 June 20X3.

	$
Balance per cash book – credit balance	4,300
Unpresented cheques	1,500
Bank charges not entered in the cash book	300
Receipts not yet credited by the bank	2,600
Dishonoured cheques not yet recorded in the cash book	500

What would be the balance shown on the bank statement at 30 June 20X3?

$ _____   _____
Favourable/overdrawn

44 Financial controls are primarily needed to

A   minimise the risk of fraud and error
B   comply with legal requirements
C   improve the efficiency of the business
D   reduce the expenses of the external auditors

45 The following information relates to NBV for the year ended 31 July 20X3.

	$'000
Direct materials	160
Direct labour	200
Prime cost	360
Carriage outwards	880
Depreciation of delivery vehicles	30
Factory indirect overheads	450
Increase in work-in-progress inventory	75
Decrease in inventory of finished goods	55

What should be the factory cost of goods completed for the year ended 31 July 20X3? ....

46 The internal auditor at ILT has noticed that cheques from customers are being paid into the bank account approximately one month after the date on the cheque.

Should the internal auditor

A   instruct the cashier to pay cheques in more promptly?
B   disregard, because all cheques have been accounted for?
C   ask customers to pay more promptly?
D   inform senior management there may be a fraud?

47 Which of the following tests carried out by an external auditor is a compliance test?

A   Confirming authorisation of a reconciliation of the sales ledger control account
B   Checking unpresented cheques in a bank reconciliation
C   Checking a purchase invoice with the purchase day book
D   Inspecting physical existence of non-current assets

48. The following information relates to CFS:

	$'000
Machinery	
Cost at 1 January 20X2	80
Additions	20
Disposal	(10)
Cost at 31 December 20X2	90
Provision for depreciation at 1 January 20X2	15
Depreciation charge	8
Disposal	(6)
Provision for depreciation at 31 December 20X2	17

The proceeds on disposal of the machine were $1,000.

CFS is preparing the statement of cash flows for the year ended 31 December 20X2. In relation to the items above, what should be the net adjustment to operating profit in order to determine the net cash flow from operating activities?

A   Deduct $11,000
B   Add back $3,000
C   Add back $5,000
D   Add back $11,000

49. Which ONE of the following attributes is the most important for any code to possess in order to be of use in an accounting system?

A   Easy to change the code number
B   Each code is a unique number
C   A combination of letters and digits to ensure input accuracy
D   Linked to assets, liabilities, income, expenditure and capital

50. The accountant at S is preparing quarterly accounts for Quarter 3. In Quarter 2, he had accrued $1,600 for gas and this balance was carried forward to Quarter 3. In Quarter 3, a gas bill of $2,700 was paid. The accountant has accrued $2,400 for gas in Quarter 3.

What should be the charge for gas in the income statement for Quarter 3?

A $1,900
B $2,400
C $2,700
D $3,500

Mock assessment 1
Answers

1   D   A method of controlling petty cash.

2   C   Only limited companies above a certain size are required to have an external audit.

3   A

RENT PAYABLE

	$		$
Rent paid	4,000	Balance b/d – accrual	300
		Income statement charge	3,300
		Balance c/d – prepayment	
		(1,200 × 1/3)	400
	4,000		4,000

4   D   This is part of their stewardship function.

5   C

	$
1 Jan – 30 June (12,000 × 6/12)	6,000
1 July – 31 Dec (13,200 × 6/12)	6,600
	12,600

6    $ 1,150 overdrawn

	$
Bank statement balance	1,000 o/d
Less: bank charges	(100)
Add: unpresented cheques	750
Less: outstanding deposits	(500)
Balance per cash book	1,150 o/d

7   B   Only direct production costs are included in prime cost.

8    $19,000

RECEIVABLES CONTROL ACCOUNT

	$		$
Sales	250,000	Bank	225,000
Unpaid cheque	3,500	Returns	2,500
		Bad debts	3,000
		Contra	4,000
		Balance c/d	19,000
	253,500		253,500

9   A

	$
Cost	1,000
Selling price	1,200
Less: modification costs	(150)
Less: selling costs	(100)
Net realisable value	950

10 B This is normally carried out by internal auditors.

11 C The non-current asset register should agree with the nominal ledger but will not necessarily always agree if there are either errors in the register or in the nominal ledger.

12 A Annual depreciation $= \dfrac{\$120,000 - 4,000}{4 \text{ years}}$

$= \$29,000$

Depreciation charge 1 Oct – 31 Dec $= \$29,000 \times 3/12$
$= \$7,250$

13 C

	$
Output sales tax ($90,000 × 10%)	9,000
Input sales tax ($72,000 × 10%)	(7,200)
	1,800 payable

14 D True and fair is mainly determined by compliance with GAAP

15 D

SUBSCRIPTIONS ACCOUNT

	$		$
Income and expenditure a/c	9,900	Balance b/d – subs in advance	500
Balance c/d – subs in advance	600	Bank	10,000
	10,500		10,500

16 A Employer's NI contributions are not deducted from gross salaries – they are an additional cost.

17 C An internal control procedure designed to prevent certain types of fraud.

18 24% Return on capital employed = Net profit % × asset turnover
= 12% × 2
= 24%

19 D It is entirely possible that a coding system would identify the department and product to which the transaction relates as well as the nominal ledger code for posting. The department and product codes would be of most use for management accounting purposes.

20   B

NON-CURRENT ASSETS AT COST

	$'000		$'000
Balance b/d	25	Disposal	10
Additions (bal fig)	15	Balance c/d	30
	40		40

	$'000
Disposal – net book value	2
Profit on disposal	2
Proceeds	4

Net cash inflow   = $15,000 – 4,000
                   = $11,000

21   A   B and C will not give rise to any numerical imbalance.

22   D   The sales day book.

23   C

CASH ACCOUNT

	$		$
Balance b/d	300	Bankings (50,000 – 5,000)	45,000
		Wages	12,000
		Drawings	24,000
Takings (bal fig)	81,100	Balance c/d	400
	81,400		81,400

24   D   A suspense account is a location where some accumulated errors may be recorded, but it is not a method of detecting errors.

25   B   Dividends are an appropriation. All of the others are expenses of the business.

26       $22,400

        ($30,000 – $3,600 – $4,000)

27       $3,500

	$
Cash book balance	(2,200)
Bank charges	(300)
Dishonoured cheque	(400)
Amended cash book balance	(2,900)
Unpresented cheques	600
Outstanding lodgements	(1,200)
Bank statement balance	(3,500)

28       $25,000

        $10,000 + ($36,000 × 5/12) = $25,000

29 $21,000

$36,000 × 7/12 = $21,000

30 $25,000

$$\text{Annual depreciation} = \frac{\$40,000 - \$10,000}{6}$$

$$= \$5,000$$

4 years depreciation = $20,000

	$
Net book value in Dec 2001 = $40,000 − $20,000	20,000
Disposal proceeds	15,000
Loss on disposal	5,000

Total depreciation and loss on disposal = $20,000 + $5,000
                                        = $25,000

31 $1,600

	$
DEF balance	2,000
Additional invoice	2,000
Amended balance	4,000
M Ltd balance	3,000
Less: cheque payment	(600)
	2,400

Difference remaining = $4,000 − $2,400
                     = $1,600

32 $50,000

Receivables account

	$		$
Opening balance	80,000	Contra	6,000
Sales	90,000	Cheques received	100,000
		Returns inwards	4,000
		Discounts allowed	10,000
		Closing balance	50,000
	170,000		170,000

33 $299,000

	$
Net wages	240,000
Employee's tax	24,000
Employee's NI	12,000
Pension scheme contributions	6,000
Charitable donations	3,000
Gross wages	285,000
Employer's NI	14,000
	299,000

34	$6.00	
	Opening inventory	20 units @ $4.00
	Day 5 sale	15 units costing $4.00
	Remaining	5 units @ $4.00
	Day 10 purchase	8 units @ $6.00
	Day 14 sale	5 units @ $4.00
		7 units @ $6.00
	Remaining	1 unit @ $6.00

35   37.5%

Return on capital employed $= \dfrac{\text{Operating profit}}{\text{Share captial} + \text{reserves}} \times 100$

$$= \dfrac{1{,}500}{4{,}000} \times 100$$

$$= 37.5\%$$

36   1.67 : 1

Non-current asset turnover ratio $= \dfrac{\text{Turnover}}{\text{Non-current assets}}$

$$= \dfrac{5{,}000}{3{,}000}$$

$$= 1.67 : 1$$

37   3.8 : 1

Quick ratio $= \dfrac{\text{Current assets} - \text{inventory}}{\text{Current liabilities}}$

$$= \dfrac{1{,}250 - 300}{250}$$

$$= 3.8 : 1$$

38   Balance = $2,400

	A JONES			
	$			$
15.10 Returns	500	1.10	Purchases	3,500
25.10 Bank	3,000	18.10	Purchases	2,400
31.10 Balance c/d	2,400			
	5,900			5,900

39   Tanwir's capital = $38,700

	$
Cash introduced on 1 October 20X9	20,000
Car introduced	6,000
Profit for the year	17,500
Petrol paid for privately	650
Drawings	(5,000)
Home phone bill	(450)
Capital at the year end	38,700

40   The accounting concept which governs the treatment of capital is the entity concept. The entity concept ensures that the business is treated as a separate entity. Therefore every transaction made by Tanwir which affects the business must be recorded.

41   B A business is normally said to have earned revenue when the customer becomes legally obliged to pay for goods and services. Cash can be received in advance, in which case the revenue has not yet been earned.

42   C Internal auditors may also undertake value-for-money audits and support the external auditors, but their main job is to report to management on the accounting system

43       $6,200 overdrawn

	$
Balance per cash book	(4,300)
Unpresented cheques	1,500
Bank charges not entered in the cash book	(300)
Receipts not yet credited by the bank	(2,600)
Dishonoured cheques not yet recorded in the cash book	(500)
Balance per bank statement	(6,200)

44   A While financial controls are of use in all of these areas, their **primary** function is to minimise the risk of fraud and error.

45       $735,000

	$'000
Prime cost	360
Factory indirect overheads	450
Increase in inventory – work in progress	(75)
Factory cost of goods completed	735

46   D Late payment of customer cheques suggests that a fraud such as 'teeming and lading' could be taking place.

47   A This is a compliance test. The others are substantive tests.

48   D

	$'000	$'000
Loss on sale of machinery		
Net book value (10 – 6)	4	
Disposal proceeds	(1)	
Loss on disposal		3
Depreciation charge for the year		8
Total to add back to operating profit		11

49   B   Each code number <u>must </u>be unique or the system will be inoperable.

50   D

	$
Accrual for Quarter 2 reversed	(1,600)
Gas bill paid	2,700
Accrual Quarter 3	2,400
Charge to income statement Quarter 3	3,500

CIMA
Paper C2 (Certificate)
Fundamentals of
Financial Accounting

Mock Assessment 2

Question Paper	
Time allowed	**2 hours**
Answer ALL the questions	

DO NOT OPEN THIS PAPER UNTIL YOU ARE READY TO START UNDER EXAMINATION CONDITIONS

Answer ALL 50 questions

1   Which ONE of the following best describes the stewardship function?

    A   Ensuring high profits
    B   Managing cash
    C   Ensuring the recording, controlling and safeguarding of assets
    D   Ensuring high dividends to shareholders

2   External auditors are primarily responsible for

    A   writing a report to the shareholders expressing an opinion on the financial statements
    B   preparing the financial statements
    C   detecting errors and fraud
    D   ensuring that the accounts show a true and fair view

3   When preparing financial statements in periods of inflation, directors

    A   Must reduce asset values
    B   Must increase asset values
    C   Must reduce dividends
    D   Need make no adjustments

4   The following information relates to a bank reconciliation.

    (i)   The bank balance in the cashbook before taking the items below into account was $8,970 overdrawn.

    (ii)   Bank charges of $550 on the bank statement have not been entered in the cashbook.

    (iii)   The bank has credited the account in error with $425 which belongs to another customer.

    (iv)   Cheque payments totalling $3,275 have been entered in the cashbook but have not been presented for payment.

    (v)   Cheques totalling $5,380 have been correctly entered on the debit side of the cashbook but have not been paid in at the bank.

What was the balance as shown by the bank statement *before* taking the items above into account?

    $ [   ]   [   ]

           Favourable/overdrawn

5   W bought a new printing machine from abroad. The cost of the machine was $80,000. The installation costs were $5,000 and the employees received specific training on how to use this particular machine, at a cost of $2,000. Before using the machine to print customers' orders, a test was undertaken and the paper and ink cost $1,000.

What should be the cost of the machine in the company's statement of financial position?

6   In a manual accounting system, the most important reason for extracting a trial balance prior to preparing financial statements is that

     A   it proves the arithmetical accuracy of the ledgers.
     B   it provides a summary of the financial statements.
     C   it proves the individual ledger accounts are correct.
     D   it reveals how errors have been made.

7   JSL operates the imprest system for its petty cash with a float of $750. At the end of July, the cashier prepared a spreadsheet for the petty cash expenses with a total column and analysis columns. A cash voucher for petrol for $50 was incorrectly entered as $5 in the total column and also in one of the analysis columns in the spreadsheet. The total column was posted to the cash account, the analysis columns were posted to the relevant nominal ledger accounts and cash was drawn from the bank for the total of the cash expenditure on the spreadsheet.

The effect of this error would be

     A   a petty cash balance of $705.
     B   petrol expenses overstated by $45.
     C   an imbalance on the trial balance.
     D   a petty cash balance of $750.

8   The electricity account for the year ended 30 June 20X1 was as follows.

	$
Opening balance for electricity accrued at 1 July 20X0	300
Payments made during the year	
1 August 20X0 for three months to 31 July 20X0	600
1 November 20X0 for three months to 31 October 20X0	720
1 February 20X1 for three months to 31 January 20X1	900
30 June 20X1 for three months to 30 April 20X1	840

Which of the following is the appropriate entry for electricity?

	Accrued At 30 June 20X1	Charge to income statement year ended 30 June 20X1
A	$Nil	$3,060
B	$460	$3,320
C	$560	$3,320
D	$560	$3,420

9   The year end of M is 30 November 20X0. The company pays for its gas by a standing order of $600 per month. On 1 December 20W9, the statement from the gas supplier showed that M had overpaid by $200. M received gas bills for the four quarters commencing on 1 December 20W9 and ending on 30 November 20X0 for $1,300, $1,400, $2,100 and $2,000 respectively.

Which of the following is the correct charge for gas in M plc's income statement for the year ended 30 November 20X0?

     A $6,800

B $7,000

C $7,200

D $7,400

---

10   S & Co. sell three products – Basic, Super and Luxury. The following information was available at the year end.

	Basic $ per unit	Super $ per unit	Luxury $ per unit
Original cost	6	9	18
Estimated selling price	9	12	15
Selling and distribution costs	1	4	5
	units	units	units
Units of inventory	200	250	150

The value of inventory at the year end should be.................................

---

11   A car was purchased by a newsagent business in May 20X7 for:

	$
Cost	10,000
Road tax	150
Total	10,150

The business adopts a date of 31 December as its year end.

The car was traded in for a replacement vehicle in August 20Y0 at an agreed value of $5,000.

It has been depreciated at 25% per annum on the reducing-balance method, charging a full year's depreciation in the year of purchase and none in the year of sale.

What was the profit or loss on disposal of the vehicle during the year ended December 20Y0?

$	

Profit/loss

---

12   A summary of the statement of financial position of M at 31 March 20X0 was as follows

	$'000
Total assets less current liabilities	120
Ordinary share capital	40
Share premium account	10
Retained profit	10
5% loan stock	60
	120

If the operating profit for the year ended 31 March 20X0 was $15,000, what is the return on capital employed?

A   12.5%

B   25%

C   30%

D   37.5%

13 The annual sales of a company are $235,000 including sales tax at 17.5%. Half of the sales are on credit terms; half are cash sales. The receivables in the statement of financial position are $23,500.

What are the receivable days (to the nearest day)?

14 The concept of capital maintenance is important for

A The sources of finance
B The measurement of profit
C The relationship of debt to equity
D The purchase of non-current assets

15 Internal control includes 'detect' controls and 'prevent' controls. Which of the following is a detect control?

A Signing overtime claim forms
B Matching purchase invoices with goods received notes
C Preparing bank reconciliations
D Matching sales invoices with delivery notes

16 A inventory record card shows the following details.

February 1 50 units in inventory at a cost of $40 per unit
7 100 units purchased at a cost of $45 per unit
14 80 units sold
21 50 units purchased at a cost of $50 per unit
28 60 units sold

What is the value of inventory at 28 February using the FIFO method?

17 The year end for ABC is July 20X2 and in that month a company car was stolen. The net book value of the company car was $8,000, but the company expects the insurance company to pay only $6,000. The correct journal entry to record this information was entered in the books in July 20X2. In August 20X2 the insurance company sent a cheque for $6,500.

The journal entry to record this is:

		Dr $	Cr $
A	Bank	6,500	
	Sundry receivable		6,500
B	Bank	6,500	
	Sundry receivable		6,000
	Disposal of non-current assets account		500
C	Bank	500	
	Disposal of non-current assets account		500
D	Bank	500	
	Sundry receivable		500

18   The trial balance of EHL does not balance and the debits exceed the credits by $2,300. The following errors are discovered:

- the single column manual cash book receipts column was undercast by $600;
- discount received of $400 had been debited to the interest payable account;
- the proceeds of $1,000 on the sale of a non-current asset had been credited to sales.

Following the correction of these errors, the balance on the suspense account would be

A   Cr $900
B   Cr $2,100
C   Cr $3,700
D   Dr $2,100

19   At the beginning of the year in GHI, the opening work-in-progress was $240,000. During the year, the following expenditure was incurred:

	$
Prime cost	720,000
Factory overheads	72,000
The closing work-in-progress was	350,000

The factory cost of goods completed during the year was.................................

20   In July 20X2, a company sold goods at standard sales tax rate with a net value of $200,000, goods exempt from sales tax with a value of $50,000 and goods at zero sales tax rate with a net value of $25,000. The purchases in July 20X2, which were all subject to sales tax, were $161,000, including sales tax. Assume that the rate of sales tax is 15%.

The difference between sales tax input tax and sales tax output tax is

A   Dr $9,000
B   Cr $5,850
C   Cr $9,000
D   None of these

21   After the income statement for Z had been prepared, it was found that accrued expenses of $1,500 had been omitted and that closing inventory had been overvalued by $500.

The effect of these errors is an

A   overstatement of net profit of $1,000
B   overstatement of net profit of $2,000
C   understatement of net profit of $1,000
D   understatement of net profit of $2,000

22   The cashier is reconciling his company's cash book with the bank statement at 31 March 20X3.

	$
The firm's cash book shows a debit balance of	12,350

The following information is available:

Bank charges not entered in the cash book | 170
Unpresented cheques | 4,600
Direct debit payment on the bank statement not entered in the cash book | 230
Sales receipts banked, but not credited by the bank | 9,400
A cheque from a customer which had previously been entered in the cash book when received, has been returned by the bank as 'dishonoured, and this has not been recorded in the cash book | 110

What should be stated as the bank balance in the company's statement of financial position at 31 March 20X3?

23 D is preparing the accounts for A for the year ended 31 March 20X3. The most recent gas bill received by A was dated 6 February 20X3 and related to the quarter 1 November 20X2 to 31 January 20X3, and the amount of the bill was $2,100.

Which ONE of the following ledger entries should be made in A's books at 31 March 20X3?

		Debit		Credit
A	Accruals	Nil	Gas expense	Nil
B	Gas expense	$1,400	Accruals	$1,400
C	Accruals	$1,400	Gas expense	$1,400
D	Gas expense	$2,100	Accruals	$2,100

24 The following information related to Q for the year ended 28 February 20X3:

	$
Prime cost	122,000
Factory overheads	185,000
Opening work-in-progress at 1 March 20X2	40,000
Factory cost of goods completed	300,000

The closing work-in-progress at 28 February 20X3 was.................................

25 N, which is registered for sales tax, received an invoice from an advertising agency for $4,000 plus sales tax. The rate of sales tax on the goods was 17.5%. The correct ledger entries are:

		Debit		Credit
		$		$
A	Advertising expense	4,000	Payables	4,000
B	Advertising expense	4,700	Payables	4,700
C	Advertising expense	4,700	Payables	4,000
			Sales tax account	700
D	Advertising expense	4,000	Payables	4,700
	Sales tax account	700		

26   E received an invoice for the purchase of non-current asset equipment which was credited to the correct supplier's ledger account, but debited to the equipment repairs account, instead of the equipment account.

The effect of not correcting this error on the financial statements would be:

A   Profit would be overstated and non-current assets would be understated.
B   Profit would be overstated and non-current assets would be overstated.
C   Profit would be understated and non-current assets would be overstated.
D   Profit would be understated and non-current assets would be understated.

27   H began trading on 1 July 20X1. The company is now preparing its accounts for the accounting year ended 30 June 20X2. Rent is charged for a tax year, which runs from 1 April to 31 March, and was $1,800 for the year ended 31 March 20X2 and $2,000 for the year ended 31 March 20X3. Rent is payable quarterly in advance, plus any arrears, on 1 March, 1 June, 1 September and 1 December.

The charge to H's income statement for rent for the year ended 30 June 20X2 is.................................

28   The return on capital employed for S is 24% and the net asset turnover ratio is 3 times.

What is the profit margin?

A   8%
B   28%
C   72%
D   It cannot be calculated

29   The total cost of salaries charged to a limited liability company's income statement is

A   cash paid to employees
B   net pay earned by employees
C   gross pay earned by employees
D   gross pay earned by employees, plus employer's national insurance contributions

30   The following is the aged receivables analysis for J Ltd at 30 April 20X3:

Age of debt	Less than 1 month	1-2 months	2-3 months	Over 3 months
Amount ($)	12,000	24,000	8,000	6,000

The company makes an allowance for receivables as follows:

Allowance	0%	1%	10%	30%

The allowance for receivables at 1 May 20X2 brought forward was $2,880.

The entry for bad debts in the income statement for the year ended 30 April 20X3 and the net receivables figure in the statement of financial position at that date should be:

	Income statement	SOFP
A	$40 credit	$47,160
B	$40 debit	$47,160
C	$2,840 debit	$50,000
D	$2,840 credit	$47,160

31 The prime cost of goods manufactured is the total of

A   raw materials consumed
B   raw materials consumed and direct wages
C   raw materials consumed, direct wages and direct expenses
D   raw materials consumed, direct wages, direct expenses and production overheads

32 On 1 May 20X3, E owed a supplier $1,200. During the month of May, E:

• purchased goods for $1,700 and the supplier offered a 5% discount for payment within the month
• returned goods value at $100 which had been purchased in April 20X3
• sent a cheque to the supplier for payment of the goods delivered in May

The balance on the supplier's account at the end of May 20X3 is...................................

33 The main advantage of using a receivables control account is that

A   double entry bookkeeping is not necessary
B   it helps in detecting errors
C   it helps with credit control
D   it ensures that the trial balance will always balance

34 The following information relates to J for the year ended 30 April 20X3.

	$'000
Retained profit for the year	28,000
Net cash inflow from operating activities	26,000
Dividend paid	3,000
Profit on sale of non-current assets	1,000
Proceeds on sale of non-current assets	5,000
Taxation paid	2,000
Interest paid	4,000
Payments for non-current assets	8,000
Issue of loan stock	6,000

The statement of cash flows will show

A   a decrease in cash of $13,000
B   an increase in cash of $14,000
C   an increase in cash of $20,000
D   an increase in cash of $22,000

35 Which of the following is an 'appropriation of profit' in a limited liability company?

A   Interest paid
B   Dividend paid
C   Directors' remuneration
D   Retained profit

36 N operates an imprest system for petty cash. On 1 February 20X3, the float was $300. It was decided that this should be increased to $375 at the end of February 20X3.

During February, the cashier paid $20 for window cleaning, $100 for stationery and $145 for coffee and biscuits. The cashier received $20 from staff for the private use of the photocopier and $60 for a miscellaneous cash sale.

What amount was drawn from the bank account for petty cash at the end of February 20X3?

A $185
B $260
C $315
D $375

37 The following are extracts from the financial statements for the year ended 31 January 20X3 of M:

	$'000
Issued ordinary shares of $1	200
Share premium account	50
Retained profit	25
Loan stock	80
Profit before interest for the year ended 31 January 20X3	60

What is the return on total capital employed?

38 The following information was extracted from the statements of financial position of Z at 31 December 20X2 and at 31 December 20X1:

	20X2	20X1
	$'000	$'000
Inventory	100	140
Receivables	150	130
Trade payables	125	115
Other payables	60	75

What figure should appear as part of the statement of cash flows for the year ended 31 December 20X2?

$	

Inflow/outflow

39 In order to confirm that financial statements show a true and fair view, the external auditor should ensure that the financial statements comply with

A   company law
B   accounting standards
C   generally accepted accounting principles
D   all of the above

40 S purchased equipment for $80,000 on 1 July 20X2. The company's accounting year end is 31 December. It is S's policy to charge a full year's depreciation in the year of purchase. S depreciates its equipment on the reducing balance basis at 25% per annum.

The net book value of the equipment at 31 December 20X5 should be

A   Nil
B $25,312
C $29,531
D $33,750

---

41   T purchased a machine costing $14,000 on 1 August 19X9. The company estimated that the asset had a useful life of 4 years and an expected residual value of $2,000. The company uses the straight line method of depreciation. The company's financial year end is 30 November. It is the company's policy to charge a full year's depreciation in the year of purchase and none in the year of disposal. On 1 November 20X2, the asset was sold for $4,500.

What should be the profit or loss on disposal in the year ended 30 November 20X2?

$ [   ]   [   ]

                Profit/loss

---

42   Which ONE of the following is true?

A   External auditors normally check all purchase invoices
B   External auditors should prepare the accounts
C   External auditors must follow the audit procedures prepared by the internal auditors
D   External auditors check the internal control system

---

43   The following information is an extract from the statements of financial position of DCF.

	31 August 20X3	31 August 20X2
	$'000	$'000
Inventory	20	14
Trade receivables	16	18
Bank	12	10
	48	42
Trade payables	(14)	(17)
	34	25

DCF is preparing the statement of cash flows for the year end 31 August 20X3. In relation to the items above, what should be the net adjustment to operating profit in order to determine the net cash flow from operating activities?

A   Deduct $1,000
B   Deduct $2,000
C   Deduct $7,000
D   Add back $1,000

---

44   Which of the following entries would NOT affect the agreement of the totals in the trial balance?

(i)   An invoice for $300 for rent has been omitted from the ledgers

(ii)   A cash sale has been recorded as debit cash sales, credit cash

(iii)   An invoice for vehicle expenses has been charged to the vehicle non-current asset account

(iv)   A credit note for $500 for goods returned by a customer had been recorded in the correct ledgers, but as $5,000

A   (i) only

B   (i) and (ii) only

C   (i), (ii) and (iii) only

D   All of them

---

45   Which ONE of the following is NOT an intangible non-current asset?

A   Goodwill

B   Trademark

C   Investment

D   Patent

---

46   Which ONE of the following would NOT help detect errors in a computerised accounting system?

A   The use of coding systems

B   The use of batch processing

C   The use of passwords

D   The use of control accounts

---

47   E bought computer equipment on 1 January 20X0 for $24,000 and estimated that it would have a useful life of five years and a residual value of $2,000. E uses the straight line method of depreciation. On 31 December 20X1, it now considers that the remaining life is only two years and that the residual value will be nil.

What should be the annual depreciation charge for the years ended 31 December 20X2 and 20X3?

A $2,800

B $5,500

C $6,600

D $7,600

---

48   A company has a quick (acid test) ratio of 2:1. Current assets include inventory of $10,000 and receivables of $6,000. Current liabilities are $4,000.

What is the bank balance?

$	

Debit/credit

---

49   Which of the following does NOT prevent fraud and errors?

A   Authorisation procedures

B   Organisation of staff

C   Suspense accounts

D   Reconciliations

---

50   Which ONE of the following statements is TRUE?

      A   Internal auditors report to the directors
      B   External auditors report to the directors
      C   Internal auditors are employed by the shareholders
      D   External auditors are employees of a company

Mock assessment 2
Answers

DO NOT TURN THIS PAGE UNTIL YOU HAVE
COMPLETED THE MOCK ASSESSMENT 2

1	C	The directors main responsibility is to safeguard the assets of the business.	
2	A	This is the auditors primary responsibility	
3	D	Need make no adjustments	
4		$11,200 overdrawn	

Cash book	$	Bank statement	$
Balance	(8,970)	Balance	(11,200)
Bank charges	(550)	Credit in error	(425)
		Unpresented cheques	(3,275)
		Outstanding deposits	5,380
	(9,520)		(9,520)

5    $88,000

	$
Cost of machine	80,000
Installation	5,000
Training	2,000
Testing	1,000
	88,000

6	A	It proves the arithmetical accuracy of the ledgers.
7	A	The expenditure has been understated by $45 so the cash drawn from the bank will also be $45 short, giving a balance of $705
8	C	Accrued: $560; charge to I/S $3,320

Electricity account

		$		$
			Balance b/fwd	300
20X0				
1 August	Paid bank	600		
1 November	Paid bank	720		
20X1				
1 February	Paid bank	900		
30 June	Paid bank	840		
30 June	Accrual c/d			
	($840 × ²/₃)	560	Income statement	3,320
		3,620		3,620

Note: ($840 × $2/3$)

BPP
LEARNING MEDIA

9 A $6,800

Gas supplier account

	$			$
Balance b/fwd	200			
Bank $600 × 12	7,200	28 February	Invoice	1,300
		31 May	Invoice	1,400
		31 August	Invoice	2,100
		30 November	Invoice	2,000
		30 November	Balance c/d	600
	7,400			7,400

Gas account

		$			$
28 February	Invoice	1,300			
31 May	Invoice	1,400			
31 August	Invoice	2,100			
30 November	Invoice	2,000	30 November	I/S account	6,800
		6,800			6,800

10 $4,700

	Cost	Net realisable value	Lower of cost & NRV	Units	Value
	$	$	$		$
Basic	6	8	6	200	1,200
Super	9	8	8	250	2,000
Luxury	18	10	10	150	1,500
					4,700

11 Profit: $781

	$
Cost	10,000
20X7 Depreciation	2,500
	7,500
20X8 Depreciation	1,875
	5,625
20X9 Depreciation	1,406
	4,219
20Y0 Part exchange	5,000
Profit	781

12 A 12.5% $\dfrac{\text{Operating profit}}{\text{Capital employed}} = \dfrac{\$15,000}{\$120,000} \times 100 = 12.5\%$

13 73 days $\dfrac{\text{Receivables including sales tax}}{\text{Credit sales inlcuding sales tax}} = \dfrac{\$23,500}{\$117,500} \times 365\,\text{days} = 73\,\text{days}$

14 B The measurement of profit

| 15 | C | Preparing bank reconciliations |

16      $2,950. 10 units at $45 plus 50 units at $50

| 17 | B | This receipt will eliminate the insurance receivable and reduce the loss on disposal by 500. |

18   B

Suspense account

DR	Discounts received	800	Opening balance	2,300	R
	Closing balance	2,100	Cash receipts	600	
		2,900		2,900	

Discount received should have been posted as a credit, so appears in the suspense account as DR 800

19    $682,000

Opening WIP	240,000
Prime cost	720,000
Overheads	72,000
Closing WIP	(350,000)
Factory cost of finished goods	682,000

20   C

Output tax 200,000 × 15%	(30,000)
Input tax 161,000 × 15/115	21,000
Payable	(9,000)

21   B

Missing accrual	1,500
Closing inventory overvalued – cost of sales understated	500
Net profit overstated	2,000

22    $11,840

Cash book balance	12,350
Bank charges	(170)
Direct debit	(230)
Dishonoured cheque	(110)
	11,840

23   B   Gas charges for two months have to be accrued

	DR	CR
Gas expense	1,400	
Accruals		1,400

24    $47,000

Opening WIP	40,000
Prime cost	122,000
Overheads	185,000
Factory cost of finished goods	(300,000)
Closing WIP	47,000

25 D $4,700 is payable. $700 goes to the sales tax account in the statement of financial position.

26 D   The cost of the equipment has been debited to the income statement instead of non-current assets so both profit and non-current assets are understated.

27 $1,850

1.7.20X1 – 31.3.20X2 1800 x 9/12 =	1,350
1.4.20X2 – 30.6.20X2 2000 x 3/12 =	500
	1,850

28 A   Net profit margin = ROCE / Net asset turnover
                             = 24%/3 = 8%

29 D   Remember, employers NI is an additional cost.

30 A

1-2 months	24,000 × 1%	240
2-3 months	8,000 × 10%	800
Over 3 months	6,000 × 30%	1,800
SOFP total		2,840
Provision b/f		(2,880)
Credit income statement		(40)

Total receivables	50,000
Less provision	(2,840)
	47,160

31 C   Prime cost includes all *direct* costs of production.

32 $1,100

DR		Supplier account		CR
Returns	100	Balance b/f		1,200
Payment	1,615	Goods		1,700
Discount received	85			
Balance c/f	1,100			
	2,900			2,900

33 B   It helps in detecting errors. It should agree to the sales ledger.

34 C

Net cash inflow from operating activities	26,000
Dividend paid	(3,000)
Proceeds of sale of non-current assets	5,000
Taxation paid	(2,000)
Interest paid	(4,000)
Payments for non-current assets	(8,000)
Issue of debentures	6,000
Net increase	20,000

35 B   A and C are expenses. Dividends are paid out of retained profit.

36 B

Window cleaning	20
Stationery	100
Coffee etc.	145
Staff receipt	(20)
Cash sale proceeds	(60)
Increase in float	75
	260

37 17% $\dfrac{\text{Profit before interest}}{\text{Capital} (200 + 50 + 25 + 80)}\% = \dfrac{60}{355}\% = 16.9\%$

38 $15,000 inflow

	Inflow	Outflow
Reduction in inventory	40,000	
Increase in receivables		20,000
Increase in trade payables	10,000	
Reduction in other payables		15,000
	50,000	35,000
Net inflow	15,000	

39 D Although GAAP is generally taken to include all of them.

40 B

		NBV
Purchase price		80,000
20X2	75%	60,000
20X3	75%	45,000
20X4	75%	33,750
20X5	75%	25,312

41 $500 loss

Annual depreciation on the machine : Depreciable amount (14,000 – 2,000)/4 = 12,000/4 = 3,000

	$
Cost	14,000
Depreciation – 3 years	9,000
Net book value	5,000
Proceeds of sale	(4,500)
Loss on disposal	500

42 D Part of an external audit will always be a check on the internal control system.

43 C

Increase in inventory	(6,000)
Decrease in receivables	2,000
Decrease in payables	(3,000)
Net adjustment	(7,000)

44 D All of these entries, or lack of entries, have equal postings to debit and credit, so the errors will not be detected by taking out a trial balance.

45	C	An investment is classified as a tangible non-current asset.	

46   C   Passwords will prevent, and maybe even detect, unauthorised access to the **computer** system, but would have no effect on the accounting system

47   D

	$	$
Original cost	24,000	
Residual value	(2,000)	
	22,000	
Annual depreciation (22,000 / 5)		4,400
31 December 20X1		
Original cost	24,000	
2 years depreciation	(8,800)	
	15,200	
Annual depreciation (15,200 / 2)		7,600

48   $2,000 debit

	$
Receivables	6,000
Bank	2,000
Quick assets	8,000
Current liabilities	4,000
Ratio:	2 : 1

49   C   Suspense accounts are an aid to investigating and correcting fraud and error, but will not prevent them from occurring.

50   A   Internal auditors are employees of the company and report to the directors. External auditors are employed by the shareholders and report to them.

Review Form & Free Prize Draw – Paper C2 Fundamentals of Financial Accounting (12/09)

All original review forms from the entire BPP range, completed with genuine comments, will be entered into one of three draws on 31 July 2010, 31 January 2011 and 31 July 2011. The names on the first four forms picked out on each occasion will be sent a cheque for £50.

Name: _____   Address: _____

_____

_____

How have you used this Kit?
(Tick one box only)

☐ Home study (book only)

☐ On a course: college _____

☐ With 'correspondence' package

☐ Other _____

Why did you decide to purchase this Kit?
(Tick one box only)

☐ Have used the complementary Study text

☐ Have used other BPP products in the past

☐ Recommendation by friend/colleague

☐ Recommendation by a lecturer at college

☐ Saw advertising

☐ Other _____

During the past six months do you recall seeing/receiving any of the following?
(Tick as many boxes as are relevant)

☐ Our advertisement in *CIMA Insider*

☐ Our advertisement in *Financial Management*

☐ Our advertisement in *Pass*

☐ Our brochure with a letter through the post

☐ Our website www.bpp.com

Which (if any) aspects of our advertising do you find useful?
(Tick as many boxes as are relevant)

☐ Prices and publication dates of new editions

☐ Information on product content

☐ Facility to order books off-the-page

☐ None of the above

Which BPP products have you used?

Text	☐	CD	☐	i-Learn	☐
Passcards	☐	Virtual Campus	☐	MCQ cards	☐
Kit	☑	i-Pass	☐		

Your ratings, comments and suggestions would be appreciated on the following areas.

	Very useful	Useful	Not useful
Effective revision	☐	☐	☐
Exam guidance	☐	☐	☐
Multiple choice questions	☐	☐	☐
Objective test questions	☐	☐	☐
Guidance in answers	☐	☐	☐
Content and structure of answers	☐	☐	☐
Mock assessments	☐	☐	☐
Mock assessment answers	☐	☐	☐

	Excellent	Good	Adequate	Poor
Overall opinion of this Kit	☐	☐	☐	☐

Do you intend to continue using BPP products?   Yes ☐   No ☐

The BPP author of this edition can be e-mailed at: janiceross@bpp.com

Please return this form to: Janice Ross, CIMA Certificate Publishing Manager, BPP Learning Media Ltd, FREEPOST, London, W12 8BR

Review Form & Free Prize Draw (continued)

TELL US WHAT YOU THINK

Please note any comments and suggestions/errors below

Free Prize Draw Rules

1 Closing date for 31 July 2010 draw is 30 June 2010. Closing date for 31 January 2011 draw is 30 December 2010. Closing date for 31 July 2011 draw is 30 June 2011.

2 Restricted to entries with UK and Eire addresses only. BPP employees, their families and business associates are excluded.

3 No purchase necessary. Entry forms are available upon request from BPP Learning Media Ltd. No more than one entry per title, per person. Draw restricted to persons aged 16 and over.

4 Winners will be notified by post and receive their cheques not later than 6 weeks after the relevant draw date.

5 The decision of the promoter in all matters is final and binding. No correspondence will be entered into.